the
Chinese
Travelmate

compiled by
Lexus
with
Yueshi Gu

LEXUS

Published 2005 by Lexus Ltd
60 Brook Street, Glasgow G40 2AB

Maps drawn by András Bereznay
Typeset by Elfreda Crehan
Chinese editor: Violette Zhu
English editor: Tom Mitford
Series editor: Peter Terrell

© Lexus Ltd

www.lexusforlanguages.co.uk

British Library Cataloguing in Publication Data
A catalogue record for this book is available from the
British Library.

ISBN 1-904737-06-4

Printed and bound in Great Britain by Scotprint

Your Travelmate

gives you one single easy-to-use A to Z list of words and phrases to help you communicate in Mandarin Chinese.

Built into this list are:

- travel tips (✈) with facts and figures which provide valuable information
- typical replies to some of the things you might want to ask
- language notes giving you basic information about speaking the language.

There is a menu reader on pages 77-86. There are maps of China on pages 151-153. There is a list of common Chinese signs and notices on pages 154-157. And Chinese numbers are given on pages 158-160.

To identify the key word in the translation of a phrase, italics are used for the pronunciation and blue for the Chinese character(s).

Speaking Chinese

This book uses a standard system, called Pinyin, for writing Chinese in the roman alphabet. But Pinyin itself needs some explanation before it can serve as an aid to pronunciation. A quick guide to the main points is given on each righthand page of this Travelmate. Here is a fuller breakdown.

a	as in father	ch	as in **ch**urch
ai	as in**Thailand**	e	as in h**er**
ang	h**ang**, with the a as in f**a**ther	ei	as in w**ei**ght
		en	as in op**en**
ao	as in h**ow**	eng	as in op**en** + **g**
c	ts, as in lo**ts**		

i	as in **feel**, or before a consonant as in p**in**	ua	wa
		uai	why
		ui	way
		un	as in fl**uent**
ian	yen	uo	war
ie	yeh	ü, ʊ	as in French t**u** or German **ü**
iʀ	as in s**ir**		
iu	yo	üe	as in French t**u** + e as in h**en**
o	or		
ong	on as in s**oon** + **g**	x	sh, as in **sh**eep
ou	as in s**oul**	yan	yen
q	ch, as in **ch**eese	z	dz, as in be**ds**
u	as in s**oon**	zh	j, as in **j**erk

The Chinese Travelmate makes two modifications to Pinyin. An ʀ is added after i to clarify that the **i** is as in s**ir**; u is written as ʊ when pronounced as in French **tu** or German **ü**.

Tones

Mandarin Chinese has four tones (fā, fá, fǎ, fà). And the tones determine meaning. You can think of spoken English as having tones too. But in spoken English the tones express uncertainty, surprise, anger etc (eg in the dialogue no? – no!). Chinese words are pitched, sung almost.

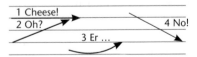

Two consecutive third tones usually change in speech to a second plus a third tone. The Travelmate shows this change and generally reflects the tone patterns of *spoken* Chinese.

A

a, an

> Chinese does not have (or need) a word
> for 'a' (or 'the'). So if you say:
>
> **wó yǒu dìtú**
>
> context will make it clear whether you
> mean
>
> I've got **a** map *or* I've got **the** map
>
> and, in any case, the literal meaning
> (*I have map*) is perfectly adequate.

about: is he about? tā zài ma? 他在吗？
  about 2 o'clock dàyūē liángdiǎn 大约两点
above zài...shàngtou 在…上头
abroad guówài 国外
absolutely! juéduì 绝对
accelerator yóumén 油门
accept jiēshòu 接受
accident shìrgù 事故
  there's been an accident chūle ge shìrgù

> ✈ The emergency number for traffic acci-
> dents is 122.

accurate zhǔnquè 准确
across: across the street jiē duìmiàn 街对
面
acupuncture zhēnjiǔ 针灸
adaptor duōyòng chātóu 多用插头
address dìzhǐr 地址
admission *(to building)* rùchǎng 入场
advance: can we book in advance? wǒmen
néng shìrxiān yùdìng ma? 我们能事先预订
吗？

advert guǎnggào 广告

Afghanistan Āfùhàn 阿富汗

afraid: I'm afraid so kǒngpà shìr zhèiyàng 恐怕是这样

 I'm afraid not kǒngpà bùxíng 恐怕不行

after zài…yǐhòu 在…以后

 (afterwards) yǐhòu

 after you nín xiān qǐng 您先请

afternoon xiàwǔ 下午

 in the afternoon xiàwǔ

 this afternoon jīntian xiàwǔ

aftershave xūhòushuǐ 须后水

again zài 再

against *(leaning on)* kàozhe 靠着

 (versus) duì 对

 (as protection) fáng 防

age niánjì 年纪

 under age wèichéngnián 未成年

 it takes ages yào yòng hěn cháng shírjiān 要用很长时间

ago: a week ago yíge xīngqī yǐqián 一个星期以前

 it wasn't long ago bùjiǔ yǐqián

 how long ago was that? nà shìr duōjiǔ yǐqián?

agree: I agree wǒ tóngyì 我同意

 it doesn't agree with me *(of food)* bù hé wǒ de wèikǒu 不合我的胃口

air kōngqì 空气

 by air *(travel)* zuò fēijī 坐飞机

 (send) kōngyùn 空运

air-conditioning kōngtiáo 空调

air hostess kōngzhōng xiáojiě 空中小姐

airmail: by airmail kōngyùn 空运

airport jīchǎng 机场

✈ You should allow plenty of time for check-in procedures, a good hour and a half for domestic flights and more for international. You're not allowed alcohol in your hand baggage on domestic flights (and possibly also on international flights). 300ml of water is the maximum allowed, and security may ask you to drink some of it.

airport bus jīchǎng bānchē 机场班车
aisle seat kào zǒuláng de zuòwèi 靠走廊的座位
alarm clock nàozhōng 闹钟
alcohol jiǔ 酒
  is it alcoholic? zhè hán *jiǔjīng* ma? 这含酒精吗？

✈ Apart from beer, the most popular alcoholic drink is **báijiǔ** 白酒 – white liquor – which is very potent!

alive: is he still alive? tā hái *huózhe* ma? 他还活着吗？
all suóyǒu 所有
  all the flights suóyǒu bānjī
  all night zhěngyè 整夜
  all day zhěngtiān 整天
  that's all jiù zhèxiē 就这些
  that's all I have wó yǒu de jiù nàme duō 我有的就那么多
  that's all wrong *wánquán* búduì 完全不对
  thank you – not at all xièxie nǐ – búyòng xiè 谢谢你—不用谢
all right hǎo 好
  it's all right méi wèntí 没问题
  I'm all right wǒ hái hǎo

c	→ ts
e	→ er
ei	→ ay
ie	→ yeh
iR	→ er
iu	→ yo
o	→ or
ou	→ oh
q	→ ch
ui	→ way
uo	→ war
x	→ sh
z	→ dz
zh	→ j

allergic: I'm allergic to... wǒ duì...guòmǐn 我对⋯过敏

allowed: is it allowed? zhè yúnxǔ ma? 这允许吗?

  that's not allowed nà shìr bù yúnxǔ de

  allow me ràng wǒ 让我

almost chàbuduō 差不多

alone yíge rén 一个人

  did you come here alone? nǐ yíge rén lái de?

  leave me alone bié lí wǒ 别理我

already yǐjing 已经

also yě 也

although suīrán 虽然

altogether yígòng 一共

  what does that make altogether? yígòng duōshao qián?

always zǒng 总

am¹ *go to* **be**

am² *(in the morning)* shàngwǔ 上午

ambulance jiùhùchē 救护车

  get an ambulance! jiào liàng jiùhùchē

> ✈ Dial 120 for an ambulance.

America Měiguó 美国

American *(person)* Měiguó rén 美国人

  (adjective) Měiguó 美国

among zài...zhōng 在⋯中

amp ānpéi 安培

  a 13 amp fuse shíRsān ānpéi de báoxiǎnsīR

and hé 和

angry shēngqì 生气

  I'm very angry (about it) nèijiàn shìR ràng wǒ hěn shēngqì

ankle jiǎobózir 脚脖子

anniversary: it's our anniversary jīntiān shìR wǒmen de *zhōunián jìniànr*R 今天是我们的周

年纪念日

annoy: he's annoying me tā zhēn ràng wǒ *fán* 他真让我烦

   it's very annoying zhēn fán rén

anorak lián mào jiákè 连帽夹克

another: can we have another room? wǒmen kéyǐ huàn *biéde* fángjiān ma? 我们可以换别的房间吗?

   another beer, please qǐng *zài* lái ge píjiǔ 请再来个啤酒

answer huídá 回答

   what was his answer? tā zěnme huídá?

   there was no answer (on phone) méi rén jiē 没人接

antibiotics kàngshēngsù 抗生素

antique gúdǒng 古董

any: have you got any bananas/butter? ní yǒu xiāngjiāo/huángyóu ma? 你有香蕉/黄油吗?

   I haven't got any wǒ méiyǒu 我没有

> Chinese doesn't use a word for 'any': **wǒ méi yǒu** simply means 'I not have'.

---

anybody rènhé rén 任何人

   is anybody here? zhèr yǒu rén ma? 这儿有人吗?

   we don't know anybody here zài zhèr wǒmen *shéi* dōu bú rènshir 在这儿我们谁都不认识

   can anybody help? *shéi* lái bāngbang máng? 谁来帮帮忙?

   I can't see anybody wǒ *shéi* yě kànbújiàn 我谁也看不见

anything shénme 什么

   anything will do shénme dōu kéyǐ

   have you got anything for...? ní yǒu shénme dōngxi gěi...?

c	→	ts
e	→	er
ei	→	ay
ie	→	yeh
iʀ	→	er
iu	→	yo
o	→	or
ou	→	oh
q	→	ch
ui	→	way
uo	→	war
x	→	sh
z	→	dz
zh	→	j

I don't want anything wǒ shénme yě bú yào

apology: please accept my apologies qǐng
jiēshòu wǒ de *dàoqiàn* 请接受我的道歉

appendicitis lánwěiyán 阑尾炎

appetite wèikǒu 胃口

I've lost my appetite wǒ méi wèikǒu

apple píngguǒ 苹果

apple pie píngguǒ pài 苹果派

appointment: can I make an appointment?
wǒ néng yūe ge shíʀjiān ma? 我能约个时间
吗?

apricot xìng 杏

April sìʀyuè 四月

area *(neighbourhood)* dìqū 地区
  (space) miànjī 面积

area code qūhào 区号

> ✈ When calling a mobile in a different city,
> add a 0 before the mobile number.

arm gēbo 胳膊

around go to **about**

arrange: will you arrange it? nǐ ānpái ma?
你安排吗?

arrest *(verb)* dàibǔ 逮捕

arrival dàodá 到达

arrive dào 到

  we only arrived yesterday wǒmen zuótiān cái
  dào

art yìshù 艺术

art gallery měishùguǎn 美术馆

arthritis guānjié yán 关节炎

artificial rénzào 人造

artist yìshù jiā 艺术家

as: as quickly as you can nǐ jìnkuài 你尽快

  as much as you can jìn ní suǒ néng 尽你所能

  as you like suí nǐ 随你

ashore zài ànshang 在岸上
  to go ashore shàng àn 上岸
ashtray yānhuī gāng 烟灰缸
Asia Yàzhōu 亚洲
ask wèn 问
  could you ask him to...? qíng nǐ *ràng tā*...
  请你让他···
  that's not what I asked for nà bú shìr wǒ yào
  de 那不是我要的
asleep: he's still asleep tā hái zài *shuìjiào* 他还
  在睡觉
asparagus lúsǔn 芦笋
aspirin āsīrpǐlín 阿斯匹林
assistant *(in shop)* shòuhuòyuán 售货员
  (helper) zhùshǒu 助手
asthma xiàochuǎn 哮喘
at: at the airport zài jīchǎng 在机场
  at one o'clock yì diǎn 一点
  at Wang's zài Wáng jiā 在王家
attitude tàidu 态度
attractive: I think you're very attractive wǒ
  juéde nǐ hén *yǒu mèilì* 我觉得你很有魅力
aubergine qiézir 茄子
August bāyuè 八月
aunt: my aunt *(father's sister)* wǒ gūgu
  我姑姑
  (mother's sister) wǒ yí 我姨
Australia Àodàlìyà 澳大利亚
Australian *(person)* Àodàlìyà rén 澳大利
  亚人
  (adjective) Àodàlìyà 澳大利亚
authorities guānfāng 官方
automatic zìrdòng 自动
autumn: in the autumn qiūtiān 秋天
away: is it far away from here? lí zhèr
  yuǎn ma? 离这儿远吗？

c	→ ts
e	→ er
ei	→ ay
ie	→ yeh
iʀ	→ yehr
iu	→ yo
o	→ or
ou	→ oh
q	→ ch
ui	→ way
uo	→ war
x	→ sh
z	→ dz
zh	→ j

go away! gǔn! 滚 !
awful zāotòule 糟透了
axle zhóu 轴

B

baby yīng'ér 婴儿
　we'd like a baby-sitter wǒmen xūyào yíge kān háiziʀ de
back (of body) bèi 背
　I've got a bad back wǒ de bèi bù hǎo
　at the back zài hòumian 在后面
　I'll be right back wǒ jiù huílai 我就回来
　is he back? tā huílai le ma?
　can I have my money back? néng bǎ qián huángei wǒ ma? 能把钱还给我吗?
　I go back tomorrow wǒ míngtiān huíqu 我明天回去
backpacker bèibāokè 背包客
bad huài 坏
　it's not bad búcuò 不错
　too bad! (bad luck) zhēn dǎoméi! 真倒霉!
　(nothing to be done) méi bànfa! 没办法!
bag bāo 包
　(suitcase) xiāngziʀ 箱子
　(handbag) shǒutí bāo
baggage xíngli 行李
baker's miànbāofáng 面包房
balcony yángtái 阳台
　a room with a balcony dài yángtái de fángjiān
bald tūtóu 秃头
ball (football etc) qiú 球
ball-point (pen) yuánzhūbǐ 圆珠笔
bamboo zhúziʀ 竹子
bamboo shoots zhúsǔn 竹笋

banana xiāngjiāo 香蕉
band *(musical)* yuèduì 乐队
bandage bēngdài 绷带
  could you change the bandage? nín néng bāng wǒ huàn bēngdài ma?
Bangladesh Mèngjiālā 孟加拉
bank *(for money)* yínháng 银行

✈ Some banks are open seven days a week.

Bank of China Zhōngguó Yínháng 中国银行
bar jiǔbā 酒吧
  in the bar zài jiǔbā

> YOU MAY HEAR
> nǐ yào hē diǎnr shénme? *what will it be?*

barber's lǐfà diàn 理发店

✈ All hairdressers' are unisex.

bargain: it's a real bargain zhēn piányi 真便宜
barmaid fúwù yuán 服务员
barman fúwù yuán 服务员
baseball cap bàngqiú mào 棒球帽
basket lánzir 篮子
bath xǐzǎo 洗澡
  can I have a bath? wǒ néng xǐ ge zǎo ma?
  could you give me a bath towel? nǐ néng géi wǒ yìtiáo *yùjīn* ma? 你能给我一条浴巾吗？
bathroom yùshìr 浴室
  we want a room with bathroom wǒmen yào yíge yǒu yùshìr de fángjiān
  can I use your bathroom? néng yòng yíxià nǐde *wèishēngjiān* ma? 能用一下你的卫生间吗？

c	→	**ts**
e	→	**er**
ei	→	**ay**
ie	→	**yeh**
iʀ	→	**er**
iu	→	**yo**
o	→	**or**
ou	→	**oh**
ui	→	**way**
uo	→	**war**
x	→	**sh**
z	→	**dz**
zh	→	**j**

battery diànchír 电池
be

> The Chinese for 'to be' is **shìr** 是 and there is only one form of this verb: no endings, no tenses. So, for example:
>
> **wǒ shìr/wǒmen shìr**
>
> can mean
> I am/we are *or* I was/we were *or* I will be/we will be
>
> There are two important cases when Chinese does not use an equivalent for the verb 'to be'.
>
> 1. **shìr** is not normally used before adjectives.
>
> **wǒ fán le**
> I am/was bored
>
> 2. **shìr** is not usually used with **zài**.
>
> **tā zài Běijīng**
> he is/was in Beijing
>
> In the negative:
>
> **don't be...** bié... 别 …
> **don't be late** bié wǎn le

beach shātān 沙滩
  on the beach zài shātānshang
bean curd dòufu 豆腐
beans dòuzir 豆子
bean sprouts dòuyá 豆芽
beautiful měi 美
  (day) hǎo 好
  (meal) hǎochīr 好吃
  (music) hǎotīng 好听

(colour) piàoliang 漂亮

because yīnwèi 因为

   because of the weather tiānqì de *yuányīn* 天气的原因

bed chuáng 床

   a single bed dānrén chuáng

   a double bed shuāngrén chuáng

   I'm off to bed wǒ yào shàng chuáng le

   you haven't changed my bed nǐ hái méi zhénglǐ wǒ de chuáng ne

bedroom wòshìR 卧室

bee mìfēng 蜜蜂

beef niúròu 牛肉

beer píjiǔ 啤酒

   two beers, please qǐng lái liǎngbēi píjiǔ

> ✈ The price of beer can vary tremendously, from 2 or 3 yuán 元 in a simple bar to 50 yuán or more in an expat joint in a big city. Draught beer is popular in the hot Chinese summer, and is often cheaper than bottled beer. Ask for **zhā pí**.

before: before breakfast zǎofàn *yǐqián* 早饭以前

   before we leave wǒmen zǒu yǐqián

   I haven't been here before wó yǐqián méi láiguò zhèr

begin: when does it begin? shénme shírhou *kāishǐ*? 什么时候开始？

beginner chūxuézhě 初学者

behind hòumiàn 后面

   the car behind me wǒ hòumiàn de chē

believe: I don't believe you wǒ bù xiāngxìn 我不相信

   I believe you wǒ xiāngxìn nǐ

bell *(in hotel, on door)* líng 铃

c	→ ts
e	→ er
ei	→ ay
ie	→ yeh
iʀ	→ er
iu	→ yo
o	→ or
ou	→ oh
q	→ ch
ui	→ way
uo	→ war
x	→ sh
z	→ dz
zh	→ j

belong: that belongs to me nà shìʀ wǒ de
那是我的

who does this belong to? zhè shìʀ shéide?

below yǐxià 以下

below the knee qīgài yǐxià

belt yāodài 腰带

bend *(in road)* zhuǎnwān 转弯

berth *(on ship)* wòpù 卧铺

beside zài...pángbiān 在…旁边

best zuìhǎo 最好

it's the best holiday I've ever had zhè shìʀ wǒ guò de zuìhǎo de jiàqī

better gènghǎo 更好

haven't you got anything better? ní yǒu méiyǒu gènghǎo de?

are you feeling better? háo diǎnr ma? 好点 儿吗?

I'm feeling a lot better wó hǎo duō le

between zài...zhīʀjiān 在…之间

beyond guòle 过了

beyond the mountains guòle shān

Bhutan Bùdān 不丹

bicycle zìʀxíngchē 自行车

> ✈ Bicycles can be hired in all big cities and are a cheap and convenient way of getting around.

big dà 大

a big one yíge dàde

that's too big tài dà le

have you got a bigger one? ní yǒu dà diǎnr de ma? 你有大点儿的吗?

bike zìʀxíngchē 自行车

bikini bǐjīní 比基尼

bill zhàngdān 账单

could I have the bill, please? kéyǐ mǎi dān

ma? 可以买单吗？

bird niǎo 鸟

birthday shēngrìʀ 生日

  happy birthday! shēngrìʀ kuàilè!

  it's my birthday jīntiān shìʀ wǒ shēngrìʀ

biscuit bǐnggān 饼干

bit: just a little bit for me wǒ jiù yào *yìdiǎn* 我就要一点

  just a little bit jiù yìdiǎn

  that's a bit too expensive yǒu yìdiǎn guì

  a bit of that cake yìdiǎn nàge dàngāo

  a big bit yí dà kuài 一大块

bitter *(taste)* kǔ 苦

black hēi 黑

blackout: he's had a blackout tā yūndǎo le 他晕倒了

blanket tǎnziʀ 毯子

bleach *(for cleaning)* piǎobái jì 漂白剂

bleed liúxuè 流血

bless you! *(after sneeze)*

✈ Chinese people don't say anything in response to a sneeze. In Hong Kong you can say **hao-a**.

c	→ ts
e	→ er
ei	→ ay
ie	→ yeh
iʀ	→ er
iu	→ yo
o	→ or
ou	→ oh
q	→ ch
ui	→ way
uo	→ war
x	→ sh
z	→ dz
zh	→ j

blind *(cannot see)* máng 盲

blister qǐpào 起泡

blocked dǔle 堵了

blonde jīnfà de rén 金发的人

blood xuè 血

  his blood group is... tā de xuèxíng shìʀ... 他的血型是…

  I've got high blood pressure wó yǒu gāo xuèyā 我有高血压

  he needs a blood transfusion tā xūyào *shūxuè* 他需要输血

bloody: that's bloody good! nà tài

bàng le! 那太棒了!
bloody hell! *(annoyed)* gāi sǐ de! 该死的!
(amazed) tiān na! 天哪!
blouse nǚ chènshān 女衬衫
blue lánsè 蓝色
boarding pass dēngjī kǎ 登机卡
boat chuán 船
   when is the next boat to...? xià yì bān qù...
   de chuán shénme shíhou kāi?
body shēntǐ 身体
   (corpse) shītǐ 尸体
boil: do we have to boil the water? wǒmen
   bìxū yào bǎ shuǐ *zhǔ* yíxià ma? 我们必须要
   把水煮一下吗?
boiled egg zhǔ jīdàn 煮鸡蛋
boiled rice báifàn 白饭
boiled water kāishuǐ 开水
bolt *(noun)* chāxiāo 插销
bone gǔtou 骨头
   (in fish) cìr 刺
book shū 书
   can I book a seat for...? wǒ néng *dìng*...de
   zuò ma? 我能订···的座吗?
   I'd like to book a table for two wó xiǎng
   dìng liǎngge rén de zuò

YOU MAY THEN HEAR
jí diǎn? *for what time?*
nín de xìngmíng? *and your name is?*

---

booking office shòupiào chù 售票处
bookshop shūdiàn 书店
boot xuēzir 靴子
   (of car) hòubèi xiāng 后备箱
booze: I had too much booze last night zuó
   wǎn wǒ hē le tài duō de *jiǔ* 昨晚我喝了太多
   的酒

border biānjìng 边境

bored: I'm bored wǒ fán le 我烦了

boring wúliáo 无聊

born: I was born in... wǒ zài...chūshēng 我在
…出生
(date) wǒ shì … chūshēng de

borrow: can I borrow...? wǒ kéyǐ jiè...ma? 我可
以借…吗?

boss láobǎn 老板

both liǎ...dōu 俩…都
I'll take both of them wó liǎ dōu yào le

bottle píngziʀ 瓶子

bottle-opener qǐziʀ 起子

bottom *(of person)* pìgu 屁股
at the bottom of the hill zài shān jiǎo xià
在山脚下

bouncer ménwèi 门卫

bowl *(for soup etc)* wǎn 碗

box héziʀ 盒子

boy nánháir 男孩儿

boyfriend nán péngyou 男朋友

bra xiōngzhào 胸罩

bracelet shǒuzhuó 手镯

brake shāchē 刹车
could you check the brakes? nín néng
chá yíxià shāchē ma?
he didn't brake tā méi shāchē

brandy báilándì 白兰地

bread miànbāo 面包
**could we have some bread and
butter?** néng lái diǎnr miànbāo hé
huángyóu ma?
some more bread, please qǐng zài lái
diǎnr miànbāo

break *(verb)* dǎ pò 打破
I think I've broken my arm wǒ juéde

c	→ ts
e	→ er
ei	→ ay
ie	→ yeh
iʀ	→ er
iu	→ yo
o	→ or
ou	→ oh
q	→ ch
ui	→ way
uo	→ war
x	→ sh
z	→ dz
zh	→ j

wǒ gēbo *shé* le 我觉得我胳膊折了

you've broken it ní bǎ tā dǎ pò le

break into: my room has been broken into wǒ de fángjiān bèi *qiào* le 我的房间被撬了

breakable yì suì 易碎

breakdown huài le 坏了

I've had a breakdown wǒ de chē *pāomáo* le 我的车抛锚了

a nervous breakdown jīngshén shīrcháng 精神失常

breakfast zǎofàn 早饭

> ✈ Your hotel will almost certainly offer a Western-style breakfast. But check the Menu Reader on page 86 to see what a Chinese breakfast would be like.

breast xiōng 胸

breathe hūxī 呼吸

I can't breathe wó chuǎn bù liǎo qì 我喘不了气

bridge qiáo 桥

briefcase gōngwénbāo 公文包

brilliant *(person, idea)* hén hǎo 很好

brilliant! tài hǎo le! 太好了!

bring dàilai 带来

could you bring it to my hotel? nǐ néng bǎ tā dài dào wǒ zhù de fàndiàn lái ma?

Britain Yīngguó 英国

> In ordinary speech the Chinese don't make a distinction between Britain and England.

British Yīngguó 英国

the British Yīngguó rén 英国人

I'm British wǒ shìr Yīngguó rén 我是英国人

brochure shuōmíngshū 说明书

have you got any brochures about...? ní yǒu...de shuōmíngshū ma?

broken pòle 破了
(bone) shéle 折了
(not working) huàile 坏了

brooch xiōngzhēn 胸针

brother: my brother *(older)* wǒ gēge 我哥哥
(younger) wǒ dìdi 我弟弟

brown zōngsè 棕色
(tanned) shàihēi le 晒黑了

browse: can I just browse around? wǒ néng kànkan ma? 我能看看吗？

bruise *(noun)* yū shāng 淤伤

brunette zōngsè tóufa de nǚrén 棕色头发的女人

brush shuāzir 刷子
(painter's) huàbǐ 画笔

bucket tǒng 桶

Buddha Fó 佛

Buddhism Fójiào 佛教

Buddhist *(adjective)* Fójiào 佛教
(person) Fójiào tú 佛教徒

buffet zìrzhù cān 自助餐

building lóu 楼

bulb dēngpào 灯泡
the bulb's gone dēngpào huài le

bumbag yāobāo 腰包

bump: he's had a bump on the head tā tóushang zhuàng le ge bāo 他头上撞了个包

bunch of flowers huā shù 花束

bunk pù 铺

bunk beds shàngxià pù 上下铺

buoy fúbiāo 浮标

bureau de change wàihuì duìhuàn chù 外汇兑换处

c	→ ts
e	→ er
ei	→ ay
ie	→ yeh
iʀ	→ yo
iu	→ yo
o	→ or
ou	→ oh
q	→ ch
ui	→ way
uo	→ war
x	→ sh
z	→ dz
zh	→ j

> ✈ You can change money at the Bank of China 中国银行, major airports and hotels (which might only offer this service to their guests). When you change RMB back to your own currency in the Bank of China, remember to take the original slips from when you first changed money.

burglar zéi 贼

burgle: our flat's been burgled wǒmen de fángzir bèi *dào* le 我们的房子被盗了

> **they've taken all my money** tāmen bá wǒ de qián dōu ná zǒu le 他们把我的钱都拿走了

Burma Miǎndiàn 缅甸

burn: this meat is burnt zhè ròu shāohú le 这肉烧胡了

my arms are burnt wǒ gēbo shàishāng le 我胳膊晒伤了

can you give me something for these burns? ní yǒu zhìr tàngshāng de yào ma?

bus gōnggòng qìchē 公共汽车

which bus is it for...? ná liàng gōnggòng qìchē qù...? 哪辆公共汽车去…?

> ✈ Bus tickets are sold by the conductor once the journey is underway. Buses are cheap, but it can be difficult to know where to get off. Some major cities, however, have buses with recorded messages announcing the stops in both Chinese and English. Pushing and jostling is considered normal.

> **can you tell me when we get there?** dào le nǐ néng gàosu wǒ yìshēng ma? 到了你能告诉我一声吗?

business: I'm here on business wǒ lái zhèr chūchāi 我来这儿出差
none of your business! bù guān nǐ de shìr! 不关你的事！
business trip chūchāi 出差
bus station gōnggòng qìchē zǒngzhàn 公共汽车总站
bus stop chēzhàn 车站
bust xiōng 胸
   (*measurements*) xiōngwéi 胸围
busy (*streets*) rè'nao 热闹
   (*restaurant*) rén duō 人多
   (*telephone*) zhànxiàn 占线
   are you busy? nǐ máng ma? 你忙吗？
   it's very busy here zhèr rén hěn duō
but dànshì 但是
   not...but... búshì...érshì... 不是 … 而是 …
butcher's ròu diàn 肉店

> ✈ There are no butchers' shops in China, but you might find a butcher's counter in a big supermarket. Otherwise Chinese people buy meat at the market.

butter huángyóu 黄油
button kòuzir 扣子
buy: where can I buy...? zài nǎr néng mǎi...? 在哪儿能买 … ？
by: I'm here by myself zhǐyǒu wǒ yíge rén 只有我一个人
   are you by yourself? zhǐ nǐ yíge rén ma?
   can you do it by tomorrow? nǐ míngtiān yǐqián néng wánchéng ma? 你明天以前能完成吗？
   by train/car/plane zuò huǒchē/chē/fēijī 坐火车／车／飞机

c	→	ts
e	→	er
ei	→	ay
iR	→	yeh
iu	→	yo
o	→	or
ou	→	oh
q	→	ch
ui	→	way
uo	→	war
x	→	sh
z	→	dz
zh	→	j

by the trees zài shù páng 在树旁
who's it made by? shénme páizir de? 什么牌子的？
a book by... ...xiě de shū ···写的书
by Picasso Bìjiāsuǒ huà de 毕加索画的

C

cabbage juǎnxīn cài 卷心菜
cabin (on ship) chuáncāng 船仓
cable (electric) diànlǎn 电缆
café kāfēi guǎn 咖啡馆
cake dàngāo 蛋糕
calculator jìsuànqì 计算器
call: will you call the manager? nǐ néng jiào jīnglǐ ma? 你能叫经理吗？
what is this called? zhè jiào shénme?
I'll call back later (on phone) wǒ yìhuǐr zài dǎ 我一会儿再打
call box diànhuà tíng 电话亭
calligraphy shūfǎ 书法
calm lěngjìng 冷静
(sea) píngjìng 平静
calm down! bié zhāojí! 别着急！
Cambodia Jiánpǔzhài 柬埔寨
camcorder shèxiàngjī 摄像机
camera zhàoxiàngjī 照像机
camp: is there somewhere we can camp? yǒu kéyǐ yěyíng de dìfang ma? 有可以野营的地方吗？
can we camp here? kéyǐ zài zhèr yěyíng ma?
can¹: a can of beer yí guàn píjiǔ 一罐啤酒
can²: can I have...? néng géi wǒ...ma? 能给我···吗？
can you show me...? néng ràng wǒ kànkan... ma?

I can't... wǒ bù néng...

    I can't swim wǒ bú *huì* yóuyǒng 我不会游泳

Canada Jiānádà 加拿大

Canadian *(person)* Jiānádà rén 加拿大人

    (adjective) Jiānádà 加拿大

cancel: I want to cancel my booking wǒ yào qǔxiāo yùdìng 我要取消预订

    can we cancel dinner for tonight? wǒmen néng qǔxiāo jīn wǎn de fàn ma?

candle làzhú 蜡烛

can-opener guàntou qǐzir 罐头起子

Cantonese *(language)* Guǎngdōnghuà 广东话

car qìchē 汽车

    by car zuò qìchē

cards pūkè pái 扑克牌

    do you play cards? ní dǎ pái ma?

care: goodbye, take care zàijiàn, bǎozhòng 再见，保重

careful: be careful xiǎoxīn 小心

car park tíngchēchǎng 停车场

carpet dìtǎn 地毯

carrier bag dàizir 袋子

carrot húluóbo 胡萝卜

carry ná 拿

carving diāokè 雕刻

case *(suitcase)* xiāngzir 箱子

cash xiànjīn 现金

    I haven't any cash wǒ méiyǒu xiànjīn

    I'll pay cash wǒ fù xiànjīn

cash desk shōu yín tái 收银台

casino dúchǎng 赌场

> ✈ Gambling is illegal in China. Two exceptions are Macao and Hong Kong.

cassette lùyīndài 录音带

c	→	ts
e	→	er
ei	→	ay
ie	→	yeh
iʀ	→	er
iu	→	yo
o	→	or
ou	→	oh
q	→	ch
ui	→	way
uo	→	war
x	→	sh
z	→	dz
zh	→	j

cassette player lùyīnjī 录音机
cat māo 猫
catch: where do we catch the bus? wǒmen zài nǎr *shàng* chē? 我们在哪儿上车?
　he's caught a bug tā shēngbìng le 他生病了
cave shāndòng 山洞
CD CD
CD-player CD jī CD 机
ceiling fángdǐng 房顶
cellophane bōlizhǐr 玻璃纸
centigrade shèshìRdù 摄氏度

✈ C/5 x 9 + 32 = F						
centigrade	-5	0	10	15	21	30	36.9
Fahrenheit	23	32	50	59	70	86	98.4

centimetre límǐ 厘米

✈ 1 cm = 0.39 inches

central zhōngxīn 中心
　with central heating yǒu nuǎnqì 有暖气
centre zhōngxīn 中心
　how do we get to the centre? dào shìr zhōngxīn zěnme zǒu?
certain (sure) kěndìng 肯定
　are you certain? ní kěndìng ma?
certificate zhèngshū 证书
chain liànzir 链子
chair yǐzir 椅子
chambermaid nǚ fúwù yuán 女服务员
champagne xiāngbīn jiǔ 香槟酒
change (verb) huàn 换
　could you change this into RMB? nǐ néng bǎ zhè huàn chéng rénmínbì ma? 你能把这换成人民币吗?
　I haven't any change wǒ méi língqián 我没零钱

do you have change for 10 yuan? ní yǒu shír
kuài qián língqián ma?

do we have to change trains? wǒmen děi
huàn huǒchē ma?

I'd like to change my flight wó xiǎng huàn
bānjī

character (in Chinese writing) hànzìr 汉字

charge: who's in charge? zhèr shéi fùzé? 这儿
谁负责?

cheap piányi 便宜

have you got something cheaper? yǒu gèng
piányi de ma?

cheat: I've been cheated wǒ bèi piàn le 我被
骗了

check: will you check? nǐ néng chá yíxia ma?
你能查一下吗?

I've checked wǒ chá guò le

we checked in (at hotel) wǒmen rùzhù dēngjì
le 我们入住登记了

we checked out (from hotel) wǒmen tuìfáng le
我们退房了

check-in desk dēngjī fúwù tái 登机服
务台

check-in time bànlǐ dēngjī shǒuxù
shírjiān 办理登机手续时间

cheek (of face) liǎnjiá 脸颊

cheeky hòu liǎnpí 厚脸皮

cheerio huítóu jiàn 回头见

cheers (toast) gānbēi 干杯

(thanks) xièxie 谢谢

cheese nǎilào 奶酪

chef chúshīr 厨师

chemist's yàofáng 药房

cheque zhīrpiào 支票

cheque book zhīrpiào běn 支票本

chest xiōng 胸

c	→ ts
e	→ er
ei	→ ay
ie	→ yeh
iʀ	→ er
iu	→ yo
o	→ or
ou	→ oh
q	→ ch
ui	→ way
uo	→ war
x	→ sh
z	→ dz
zh	→ j

chewing gum kǒuxiāngtáng 口香糖
chicken xiǎojī 小鸡
 (meat) jīròu 鸡肉
chickenpox shuǐdòu 水豆
child háiziʀ 孩子
child minder bǎomǔ 保姆
children xiǎoháir 小孩儿
 a children's portion xiǎoháir de liàng
chin xiàba 下巴
china círqì 瓷器
China Zhōngguó 中国
Chinese *(adjective)* Zhōngguó 中国
 (language) Zhōngwén 中文
 the Chinese Zhōngguó rén 中国人
 a Chinese person Zhōngguó rén 中国人
 I don't speak Chinese wǒ bù shuō Zhōngwén
Chinese New Year chūnjié 春节
Chinese New Year's Day chūyī 初一
Chinese New Year's Eve chúxī 除夕
chips shǔtiáo 薯条
 (in casino) chóumǎ 筹码
chocolate qiǎokelì 巧克力
 a hot chocolate yì bēi rè qiǎokelì
 a box of chocolates yì hé qiǎokelì
chop *(seal)* túzhāng 图章
chopsticks kuàiziʀ 筷子
Christian name míngziʀ 名字
Christmas shèngdànjié 圣诞节
 on Christmas Eve shèngdànjié qián yè
 Happy Christmas shèngdànjié kuàilè

> ✈ Christmas isn't widely celebrated, though
>   some decorations are put up in big cities.

church jiàotáng 教堂
cider píngguójiǔ 苹果酒
cigar xʊějiā 雪茄

cigarette yān 烟
cinema diàngyǐng yuàn 电影院
circle yuánquān 圆圈
city chéngshìʀ 城市
city centre shìʀ zhōngxīn 市中心
claim *(insurance)* suǒpéi 索赔
clarify chéngqīng 澄清
clean *(adjective)* gānjing 干净
  it's not clean bù gānjing 不干净
  my room hasn't been cleaned today jīntiān wǒ de fángjiān hái méi *dǎsǎo* ne 今天我的房间还没打扫呢
clear: I'm not clear about it wǒ duì zhèige bú tài *qīngchu* 我对这个不太清楚
clever cōngmíng 聪明
climate qìhòu 气候
climber páshān de rén 爬山的人
climbing boots dēngshān xié 登山鞋
cloakroom *(for clothes)* yīmàojiān 衣帽间
clock zhōng 钟
close¹ jìn 近
  (weather) mēnrè 闷热
  is it close to...? lí...jìn ma?
  is it close? jìn ma?
close²: when do you close? nǐmen shénme shíʀhou *guānmén*? 你们什么时候关门?
closed guānmén le 关门了
cloth bù 布
  (rag) mābù 抹布
clothes yīfu 衣服
clothes peg yīfu jiā 衣服夹
cloud yún 云
clubbing: we're going clubbing wǒmen qù bèngdi 我们去蹦迪
clutch líhéqì 离合器

c → ts
e → er
ei → ay
ie → yeh
ìʀ → er
iu → yo
o → or
ou → oh
q → ch
ui → way
uo → war
x → sh
z → dz
zh → j

coach chángtú qìchē 长途汽车
coach party zuò chángtú qìchē de lǚyóu tuán 坐长途汽车的旅游团
coach trip zuò chángtú qìchē lǚyóu 坐长途汽车旅游
coast hǎibiān 海边
  at the coast zài hǎibiān
coat dàyī 大衣
cockroach zhāngláng 蟑螂
coconut milk yēzir nǎi 椰子奶
coffee kāfēi 咖啡
  a white coffee jiā niúnǎi de kāfēi
  a black coffee bù jiā niúnǎi de kāfēi

✈ Coffee is not normally on sale in Chinese restaurants, but Western-style coffee shops are now common in big cities. Most Chinese people don't drink coffee.

coin yìngbì 硬币
coke® kékǒu kělè 可口可乐
cold lěng 冷
  I'm cold wó lěng
  I've got a cold wó gǎnmào le 我感冒了
collapse: he's collapsed tā kuǎ le 他垮了
collar lǐngzir 领子
collect: I've come to collect... wǒ lái qǔ... 我来取…
colour yánsè 颜色
  have you any other colours? hái yǒu biéde yánsè ma?
comb shūzir 梳子
come lái 来
  I come from London wǒ cóng Lúndūn lái
  when is he coming? tā shénme shírhou lái?
  we came here yesterday wǒmen zuótiān lái de
  come here dào zhèr lái

come with me gēn wǒ lái

come on! kuài lái!

  oh, come on! *(disbelief)* bú huì ba! 不会吧！

comfortable shūfu 舒服

Communist Party Gòngchándǎng 共产党

company *(business)* gōngsī 公司

  you're good company nǐ shì háo huǒbànr 你是好伙伴儿

compartment *(in train)* chēxiāng 车厢

compass zhǐnánzhēn 指南针

compensation péicháng 赔偿

complain bùmǎn 不满

  I want to complain about my room wǒ duì wǒ de fángjiān hěn bù mǎnyì 我对我的房间很不满意

completely wánquán 完全

complicated: it's very complicated fēicháng fùzá 非常复杂

compulsory: is it compulsory? shì bìxū de ma? 是必须的吗？

computer diànnǎo 电脑

concert yīnyuè huì 音乐会

concussion nǎo zhèndàng 脑震荡

condition *(state)* qíngkuàng 情况
  (stipulation) tiáojiàn 条件

  it's not in very good condition qíngkuàng bú miào 情况不妙

condom bìyùn tào 避孕套

conference yántǎo huì 研讨会

confirm quèdìng 确定

confuse: you're confusing me nǐ bǎ wǒ nòng hútu le 你把我弄糊涂了

congratulations! gōngxǐ gōngxǐ! 恭喜恭喜！

conjunctivitis jiémó yán 结膜炎

conman piànziʀ 骗子

c	→ ts
e	→ er
ei	→ ay
ie	→ yeh
iʀ	→ er
iu	→ yo
o	→ or
ou	→ oh
q	→ ch
ui	→ way
uo	→ war
x	→ sh
z	→ dz
zh	→ j

connection *(travel)* liányòn 联运

conscious: he's conscious tā shénzhìʀ qīngxǐng 他神智清醒

consciousness: he's lost consciousness tā shīʀqù zhīʀjué le 他失去知觉了

constipation dàbiàn gānzào 大便干燥

consul lǐngshìʀ 领事

consulate lǐngshìʀ guǎn 领事馆

contact: how can I contact...? wó zěnme gēn...liánxì? 我怎么跟…联系？

contact lenses yǐnxíng yǎnjìng 隐形眼镜

convenient fāngbiàn 方便

cook: it's not cooked zhè méi zuò shú 这没做熟
  you're a good cook ní hěn huì zuòfàn 你很会做饭

cooker lúziʀ 炉子

cool liángkuai 凉快
  (great) kù 酷

corkscrew pútao jiǔpíng de qǐziʀ 葡萄酒瓶的起子

corner jiǎoʀ 角儿
  on the corner jiē jiǎo 街角
  in the corner zài jiǎoʀ li

correct duì 对

cosmetics huàzhuāng pǐn 化妆品

cost: what does it cost? zhè yào duōshao qián? 这要多少钱？

> **that's too much** tài guì le 太贵了
> **I'll take it** wǒ yào le 我要了

cot yīng'ér chuáng 婴儿床

cotton miánhua 棉花

cotton wool yàomián 药棉

couchette wòpù 卧铺

cough késou 咳嗽

cough sweets rùnhóutáng 润喉糖

could: could you please...? nǐ néng...? 你能…?
　could I have...? wǒ néng...?
　we couldn't... wǒmen bù néng...
country guójiā 国家
　in the country(side) zài nóngcūn 在农村
couple: a couple of... *(two)* liǎngge... 两个··
　(a few) jǐge... 几个··
courier tí xíngli de rén 提行李的人
course: of course dāngrán 当然
courtyard yuànzir 院子
cousin

Things get complicated.

male cousin	*father's side*	*mother's side*
younger than	**tángdì**	**biǎodì**
speaker	堂弟	表弟
older than	**tánggē**	**biǎogē**
speaker	堂哥	表哥
female cousin	*father's side*	*mother's side*
younger than	**tángmèi**	**biǎomèi**
speaker	堂妹	表妹
older than	**tángjiě**	**biáojiě**
speaker	堂姐	表姐

cover charge fúwù fèi 服务费
cow nǎiniú 奶牛
crab pángxiè 螃蟹
craftshop gōngyìpǐn shāngdiàn 工艺品
　商店
crap: this is crap zhè shìr lājī 这是垃圾
crash: there's been a crash zhuàng chē
　le 撞车了
crash helmet tóukuī 头盔
crazy fēng le 疯了
　you're crazy nǐ fēng le
　that's crazy nà zhēn huāngtang 那真

c	→ ts
e	→ er
ei	→ ay
ie	→ yeh
iʀ	→ er
iu	→ yo
o	→ or
ou	→ oh
q	→ ch
ui	→ way
uo	→ war
x	→ sh
z	→ dz
zh	→ j

荒唐

cream *(on milk)* nǎiyóu 奶油
   (for skin) cāliǎn yóu 擦脸油
credit card xìnyòng kǎ 信用卡

> ✈ China is a cash-based society. Your credit
> card is only likely to be of use in very
> upmarket restaurants, in big hotels and
> shopping malls. Carry cash.

crisps shǔpiàn 薯片
cross *(verb)* guò 过
crossroads shírzìr lùkǒu 十字路口
crowded yōngjǐ 拥挤
   it's crowded zhēn jǐ
cruise zuò háohuá yóulún lǚxíng 坐豪华游轮旅行
crutch *(for invalid)* guǎizhàng 拐杖
cry: don't cry bié kū 别哭
cup bēizìr 杯子
   a cup of coffee yìbēi kāfēi
cupboard guìzìr 柜子
curry gālí 咖哩
curtains chuānglián 窗帘
cushion kàodiàn 靠垫
Customs hǎiguān 海关
cut *(verb)* qiē 切
   I've cut myself wǒ huá pò le 我划破了
cycle: can we cycle there? wǒmen kéyǐ *qí chē*
   qù ma? 我们可以骑车去吗？
cyclist qí zìrxíngchē de rén 骑自行车的人

D

dad: my dad wǒ bàba 我爸爸
damage: I'll pay for the damage wǒ fù *sǔnshīr*
   fèi 我付损失费
damaged sǔnhuài le 损坏了

damn! tāmāde! 他妈的！

damp cháo 潮

dance: would you like to dance? ní xiǎng tiàowǔ ma? 你想跳舞吗？

dangerous wēixiǎn 危险

dark hēi 黑

  when does it get dark? tiān shénme shírhou hēi?

  dark blue shēn lán 深蓝

darling qīn'àide 亲爱的

date: what's the date? jīntiān jǐ hào? 今天几号？

  can we make a date? (romantic) wǒmen dìng ge yuēhuì shírjiān ba? 我们定个约会时间吧？

To say the date in Chinese the word order is month – number – **hào**. For years the order is number – **nián**.

the first of March sānyuè yī hào 三月一号

on the fifth of May zài wǔyuè wǔ hào

in 2004 zài èr líng líng sìr nián 在2004年

---

dates (fruit) zǎo 枣

daughter: my daughter wó nǚ'ér 我女儿

day tiān 天

  the day after dì'èr tiān

  the day before qián yì tiān

dead sǐr le 死了

deaf lóng 聋

deal: it's a deal jiù zhème dìng le 就这么定了

  will you deal with it? nǐ chúlǐ yíxià ba? 你处理一下吧？

dear (expensive) guì 贵

c → ts
e → er
ei → ay
ie → yeh
iʀ → er
iu → yo
o → or
ou → oh
q → ch
ui → way
uo → war
x → sh
z → dz
zh → j

If you're attempting a Chinese postcard, then just put the person's name without any word for 'dear'.

December shír'èryuè 十二月

deck (of ship) jiábǎn 甲板

deckchair zhédié yǐ 折叠椅

declare: I have nothing to declare wǒ méi yǒu xūyào bàoguān de dōngxi 我没有需要报关的东西

deep shēn 深

deep-fry zhá 炸

delay: the flight was delayed fēijī wándiǎn le 飞机晚点了

deliberately gùyì 故意

delicate (person) xiáoqiǎo 小巧

delicious hǎochīr 好吃

de luxe háohuá 豪华

dentist yáyī 牙医

YOU MAY HEAR
zhāng dà zuǐ *open wide*
qǐng shù zuǐ *rinse out please*
něige yá yǒu wèntí? *which tooth is the problem?*

---

dentures jiǎyá 假牙

deny: I deny it wǒ bù chéngrèn 我不承认

deodorant chúchòu jì 除臭剂

departure chūfā 出发

(of plane) qǐfēi 起飞

departure lounge hòujī shìr 侯机室

depend: it depends kàn qíngkuàng zài shuō 看情况再说

   it depends on... nà yào kàn... 那要看 …

deposit yājīn 押金

   do I have to leave a deposit? wǒ bìxū yào

jiāo yājīn ma?

depressed yùmèn 郁闷

depth shēndù 深度

desperate: I'm desperate for a drink wǒ tèbié xiǎng hē yì bēi 我特别想喝一杯

dessert tiándiǎn 甜点

destination mùdìdì 目的地

detergent xǐjié jì 洗洁剂

detour ràoxíng dào 绕行道

develop: could you develop these? nǐ néng bǎ zhèixiē xǐ le ma? 你能把这些洗了吗?

diabetic tángniào bìng 糖尿病

diamond zuànshí 钻石

diarrhoea lā dùzi 拉肚子

have you got something for diarrhoea? ní yǒu zhì lā dùzir de yào ma?

diary rìjì 日记

dictionary cídiǎn 词典

die sǐ 死

diesel cháiyóu 柴油

diet yǐnshí 饮食

I'm on a diet wǒ zài jiéshí 我在节食

different bùtóng 不同

different: they're different tāmen bùtóng

can I have a different room? wǒ néng yào lìngwài yíge fángjiān ma? 我能要另外一个房间吗?

difficult nán 难

dining room cāntīng 餐厅

dinner (evening) wǎnfàn 晚饭

dinner jacket yè lǐfú 夜礼服

direct (adjective) zhíjiē 直接

does it go direct? zhè zhídá ma? 这直达吗?

dirty zāng 脏

c	→ ts
e	→ er
ei	→ ay
ie	→ yeh
iR	→ yo
iu	→ yo
o	→ or
ou	→ oh
q	→ ch
ui	→ way
uo	→ war
x	→ sh
z	→ dz
zh	→ j

disabled cánjí 残疾

disappear bújiàn le 不见了

  it's just disappeared tā jiù bújiàn le

disappointing bù zěnmeyàng

disco dísīrkē 迪斯科

discount dǎ zhé 打折

disgusting ěxīn 恶心

dish (food) cài 菜

  (plate) pánzir 盘子

dishonest bù chéngshír 不诚实

disinfectant xiāodú jì 消毒剂

disposable camera yícìrxìng zhàoxiàng jī 一次性照相机

distance jòlí 距离

  in the distance zài yuǎnchù 在远处

disturb: the noise is disturbing us zhè zàoyīn yíngxiǎng dào wǒmen le 这噪音影响到我们了

diving board tiàobǎn 跳板

divorced líhūn 离婚

do zuò 做

  what are you doing tonight? jīnwǎn nǐ zuò shénme?

  how do you do it? gāi zěnme zuò?

  will you do it for me? nǐ néng bāng wǒ zuò yíxia ma?

  I've never done it before wó yǐqián cónglái méi zuò guo

  he did it (it was him) shìr tā 是他

  how do you do? ní hǎo 你好

doctor yīshēng 医生

  I need a doctor wǒ xūyào yíge yīshēng

✈ Big hotels usually offer medical help. There are no family doctors in China, so you'll have to go to a hospital. Some pharmacies will also diagnose and prescribe.

> *YOU MAY HEAR*
>
> nǐ yào xīyào háishìʀ zhōngyào? *do you want Western or Chinese medicine?*
> ní yǐqián yǒu zhè bìng ma? *have you had this before?*
> nǎr téng? *where does it hurt?*
> nǐ chīʀ shénme yào? *are you taking any medication?*
> chīʀ yī/liǎng piànr *take one/two of these*
> měi sānge xiǎoshír *every three hours*
> měi tiān *every day*
> yì tiān chīʀ liǎng cìr *twice a day*

document wénjiàn 文件
dog gǒu 狗
don't! bié! 别！; *go to* **not**
door mén 门
dosage jìliàng 计量
double room shuāngrén jiān 双人间
double whisky shuāngfèn wēishìʀjì 双份威士忌
down: down there nà xiàmian 那下面
  get down! xiàlai! 下来！
  it's just down the road yìzhíʀ zǒu jiù dào le 一直走就到了
downstairs lóuxià 楼下
dragon lóng 龙
drain *(noun)* xiàshuǐdào 下水道
drawing pin túdīng 图钉
dress *(woman's)* liányīqún 连衣裙
dressing *(for cut)* bēngdài 绷带
  (for salad) jiàng 酱
drink *(verb)* hē 喝
  (alcoholic) jiǔ 酒
  something to drink hē de dōngxi
  would you like a drink? nǐ yào hē diǎn shénme?

c	→	**ts**
e	→	**er**
ei	→	**ay**
ie	→	**yeh**
iʀ	→	**er**
iu	→	**yo**
o	→	**or**
ou	→	**oh**
q	→	**ch**
ui	→	**way**
uo	→	**war**
x	→	**sh**
z	→	**dz**
zh	→	**j**

I don't drink wǒ bú huì hē jiǔ
drinkable: is the water drinkable? zhè shuǐ *kéyi
hē* ma? 这水可以喝吗?

✈ Tap water is not for drinking.

drive kāichē 开车
driver sījīr 司机
driving licence jiàshǐr zhírzhào 驾驶执照
drown: he's drowning tā yào yān sǐr le 他要淹
死了
drug yào 药
　(*narcotic etc*) dúpǐn 毒品
drug dealer dúpǐn fàn 毒品犯
drunk (*adjective*) hēzuìle 喝醉了
dry (*adjective*) gān 干
dry-clean gānxǐ 干洗
dry-cleaner's gānxǐ diàn 干洗店
duck yā 鸭
due: when's the bus due? gōnggòng qìchē
jídiǎn lái? 公共汽车几点来?
during zài...de shírhou 在…的时候
dust huī 灰
duty-free shop miǎnshuì shāngdiàn 免税商店
DVD DVD
DVD-player DVD jī DVD 机

E

each: can we have one each? wǒmen kéyǐ
méizhǒng yào *yígè* ma? 我们可以每种要一
个吗?
　how much are they each? yígè yào duōshao
qián? 一个要多少钱?
ear ěrduo 耳朵
　I've got earache wó ěrduo téng
early zǎo 早

we want to leave a day earlier wǒmen yào tíqián yìtiān zǒu 我们要提前一天走

earring ěrhuán 耳环

east dōng 东

East China Sea Dōnghǎi 东海

Easter fùhuójié 复活节

easy róngyì 容易

eat chīr 吃

  something to eat chīr xiē dōngxi

egg jīdàn 鸡蛋

either: either...or... búshìr...jiùshìr... 不是 … 就是 …

  I don't like either wó *nǎge* yě bù xǐhuan 我哪个也不喜欢

elastic sōngjǐndài 松紧带

elastic band xiàngpí jīnr 橡皮筋儿

elbow gēbo zhǒu 胳膊肘

electric diàn 电

electric fire diàn lúzir 电炉子

electrician diàngōng 电工

electricity diàn 电

> ✈ You'll find both two-pin and three-pin sockets, square and round. So take an adaptor. Voltage is 220 volts as in the UK.

elegant yōuyǎ 优雅

else: something else *biéde* dōngxi 别的东西

  somewhere else biéde dìfang

  who else? hái yǒu shéi 还有谁

  or else fǒuzé 否则

email diànzǐr yóujiàn 电子邮件

  why don't you email me? nǐ wèishénme bù géi wǒ fā diànzǐr yóujiàn

c	→	ts
e	→	er
ei	→	ay
ie	→	yeh
ıʀ	→	er
iu	→	yo
o	→	or
ou	→	oh
q	→	ch
ui	→	way
uo	→	war
x	→	sh
z	→	dz
zh	→	j

email address diànzǐr xìnxiāng 电子信箱
  what's your email address? nǐ de diànzǐr xìnxiāng shìr shénme?

> *YOU MAY THEN HEAR*
> **my email address is...**
> **at...dot...**
> wǒ de diànzǐr xìnxiāng shìr...
> quān ēi...diǎnr...

embarrassed bù hǎoyìsir 不好意思
embarrassing shìr rén bù hǎoyìsir 使人不好意思
embassy dàshǐrguǎn 大使馆
emergency jǐnjí qíngkuàng 紧急情况

> ✈ Emergency numbers: 110 for the police, 120 for an ambulance, 119 for fire.

emperor huángdì 皇帝
empty kōng 空
end *(of road)* jìntóu 尽头
  (of film) jiéwěi 结尾
  (of holiday) zuìhòu 最后
  when does it end? shénme shírhou jiéshù? 什么时候结束?
engaged *(telephone)* zhànxiàn 占线
  (toilet) yǒurén 有人
  (person) dìnghūn 订婚
engagement ring dìnghūn jièzhir 订婚戒指
engine *(of car, plane)* fādòngjī 发动机
engine trouble fādòngjī wèntí 发动机问题
England Yīngguó 英国
English Yīngguó 英国
  (language) Yīngyǔ 英语
  the English Yīngguó rén 英国人
Englishman Yīngguó nánrén 英国男人
Englishwoman Yīngguó nǔrén 英国女人

enjoy: I enjoyed it very much wǒ *wánr* de hěn kāixīn 我玩儿得很开心

  enjoy yourself hǎohāo wánr

  I enjoyed the meal wǒ chīr de hǎo 我吃得好

enlargement (photo) fàngdà 放大

enormous dàjíle 大极了

enough gòu 够

  that's not big enough bú gòu dà

  I don't have enough money wǒ de qián bú gòu

  thank you, that's enough gòu le, xièxie

en suite: is it en suite? shìr yǒu wèishēngjiān de fángjiān ma? 是有卫生间的房间吗?

entertainment yúlè 娱乐

entrance rùkǒu 入口

envelope xìnfēng 信封

error cuòwù 错误

escalator zìrdòng fútī 自动扶梯

especially tèbié shìr 特别是

essential bìyào 必要

e-ticket diànzǐr jīpiào 电子机票

euro Ōuyuán 欧元

Europe Ōuzhōu 欧洲

even: even the British shènzhìr lián Yīngguó rén dōu 甚至连英国人都

evening wǎnshang 晚上

  in the evening wǎnshang

  this evening jīntian wǎnshang

  good evening wǎnshang hǎo

evening dress (for man, woman) wán lǐfú 晚礼服

ever: have you ever been to...? nǐ qùguo...ma? 你去过…吗?

Everest Zhūmùlángmǎfēng 珠穆朗玛峰

every měi 每

  every day měitiān

c	→ ts
e	→ er
ei	→ ay
ie	→ yeh
iʀ	→ er
iu	→ yo
o	→ or
ou	→ oh
q	→ ch
ui	→ way
uo	→ war
x	→ sh
z	→ dz
zh	→ j

everyone měige rén 每个人

everything měijiàn shìr 每件事

everywhere měige dìfang 每个地方

exact zhènghǎo 正好

example lìzir 例子

  for example lìrú 例如

excellent hǎojíle 好极了

except: except me chú le wǒ 除了我

excess baggage chāozhòng de xíngli 超重的
  行李

exchange rate duìhuàn lǜ 兑换率

excursion yóulǎn 游览

excuse me (to get past, get attention) láojià 劳驾
  (to apologize) duìbuqǐ 对不起

exhausted lèijíle 累极了

exhibition zhánlǎn 展览

exit chūkǒu 出口

expect: she's expecting tā huáiyùn le 她怀孕了

expenses: it's on expenses shìr gōngfèi 是公费

expensive guì 贵

  that's too expensive tài guì le

expert zhuānjiā 专家

explain jiěshìr 解释

  would you explain that slowly? nǐ néng
  màndiǎnr jiěshìr ma？

express (mail) kuàidì 快递

extension cable jiā cháng diànxiàn 加长电线

extra: an extra day éwài yìtiān 额外一天

  is that extra? yào éwài shōufèi ma？

extremely fēicháng 非常

eye yǎnjing 眼睛

eyebrow méimao 眉毛

eyebrow pencil méibǐ 眉笔

eyeliner yǎnxiàn bǐ 眼线笔

eye shadow yányǐng 眼影

eye witness jiànzhèngrén 见证人

F

face liǎn 脸
fact shìrshír 事实
factory gōngchǎng 工厂
Fahrenheit huáshìr 华氏

✈ F - 32 x 5/9 = C

Fahrenheit	23	32	50	59	70	86	98.4
centigrade	-5	0	10	15	21	30	36.9

faint: she's fainted tā yōndǎo le 她晕倒了
fair (fun-) yóulèyuán 游乐园
  (commercial) zhǎnhuì 展会
  that's not fair zhè bù gōngping 这不公平
fake (noun) jiǎhuò 假货
fall: he's fallen tā shuāidǎo le 他摔倒了
false jiǎ 假
false teeth jiǎyá 假牙
family jiātíng 家庭
family name xìng 姓
fan (cooling) fēngshàn 风扇
  (hand-held) shànzir 扇子
  football fan zúqiú mí 足球迷
far yuǎn 远
  is it far? yuǎn ma?
  how far is it? yǒu duō yuǎn?
fare (travel) chēfèi 车费
  (plane) jīpiàofèi 机票费
farm nóngchǎng 农场
farther gèng yuǎn 更远
fashion shírzhuāng 时装
fast (adjective) kuài 快
  don't speak so fast bié shuō de tài kuài
fat (adjective) pàng 胖

c	→ ts
e	→ er
ei	→ ay
ie	→ yeh
iʀ	→ er
iu	→ yo
o	→ or
ou	→ oh
q	→ ch
ui	→ way
uo	→ war
x	→ sh
z	→ dz
zh	→ j

father: my father wǒ fùqin 我父亲

fault (defect) máobing 毛病

  it's not my fault bú shìʀ wǒ de cuò 不是我的错

faulty yǒu máobing 有毛病

favourite (adjective) zuì xǐhuan 最喜欢

fax chuánzhēn 传真

  can you fax this for me? nǐ néng wèi wǒ fā zhèige chuánzhēn ma? 你能为我发这个传真吗?

February èryuè 二月

fed-up: I'm fed-up wǒ shòu gòu le 我受够了

feel: I feel like... (I want) wó xiǎng... 我想···

ferry dùchuán 渡船

fetch: will you come and fetch me? nǐ néng lái jiē wǒ ma? 你能来接我吗?

fever fāshāo 发烧

few: only a few jiù jǐ ge 就几个

  a few days jǐ tiān 几天

fiancé wèihūn fū 未婚夫

fiancée wèihūn qī 未婚妻

fiddle: it's a fiddle zhè shìʀ ge piàn jú 这是个骗局

field tiándì 田地

  (grassy) cǎodì 草地

fifty-fifty yíbàn yíbàn 一半一半

figure (number) shùzìʀ 数字

  (of person) tǐxíng 体形

fill: to fill in a form tián zhāng biǎo 填张表

fillet ròupiàn 肉片

filling (in tooth) bǔ yá 补牙

film (for camera) jiāojuǎn 胶卷

  (at cinema) diànyǐng 电影

  do you have this type of film? ní yǒu zhèizhǒng jiāojuǎn ma?

filter (for coffee) guòlǜzhǐʀ 过滤纸

  (for camera) lǜsèjìng 滤色镜

find zhǎodào 找到

if you find it rúguó ní zhǎodào de huà

I've found a... wó zhǎodào le gè...

fine (weather) hǎo 好

  OK, that's fine xíng 行

  a 50 yuan fine fákuǎn wǔshír yuán 罚款五十元

finger shóuzhǐrtou 手指头

fingernail zhǐrjia 指甲

finish: I haven't finished wǒ hái méi wán ne 我还没完呢

  when does it finish? shénme shírhou wán? 什么时候完？

fire huǒ 火

  (blaze: house on fire etc) huǒzāi

  (heater) lúzir 炉子

  fire! zháohuǒ le!

  can we light a fire here? wǒmen néng zai zhèr diánhuǒ ma?

fire brigade xiāofángduì 消防队

> ✈ Dial 119.

fire extinguisher mièhuǒ qì 灭火器

first dìyī 第一

  I was first wǒ dìyī

first aid jíjiù 急救

first aid kit jíjiù xiāng 急救箱

first class (travel) tóuděng 头等

first name míngzir 名字

> ✈ The Chinese put the surname first. So in **Wáng Huá** 王华, **Wáng** 王 is the surname and **Huá** 华 the first name.

fish yú 鱼

fit (healthy) jiànkāng 健康

  (physically) qiángzhuàng 强壮

c	→	ts
e	→	er
ei	→	ay
ie	→	yeh
iʀ	→	er
iu	→	yo
o	→	or
ou	→	oh
q	→	ch
ui	→	way
uo	→	war
x	→	sh
z	→	dz
zh	→	j

it doesn't fit me zhè duì wǒ bù *héshìr* 这对我不合适

fix: can you fix it? *(repair)* nǐ néng *xiū* ma? 你能修吗？

fizzy yǒuqìr 有汽儿

flag qí 旗

   national flag guóqí 国旗

flash *(photography)* shǎnguāngdēng 闪光灯

flat *(adjective)* píng 平

   (apartment) dānyuán fáng 单元房

   I've got a flat (tyre) wǒ de chētāi *biě* le 我的车胎瘪了

flavour wèidào 味道

flea tiàozao 跳蚤

flies *(on trousers)* kùzir lāliàn 裤子拉链

flight hángbān 航班

flight number hángbān hào 航班号

flirt *(verb)* tiáoqíng 调情

floor dìbǎn 地板

   on the second floor zài sān *céng* 在三层

✈ The ground floor is called the first floor.

flower huā 花

flu liúgǎn 流感

fly *(insect)* cāngying 苍蝇

   (go by plane) fēi 飞

foggy yǒu wù 有雾

   it's foggy yǒu wù

follow gēnzhe 跟着

   (road) yánzhe 沿着

food shíwù 食物

   (groceries) shípǐn 食品

   we'd like to eat Chinese-style food wǒmen yào chīr zhōngcān 我们要吃中餐

food poisoning shíwù zhòngdú 食物中毒

fool shǎguā 傻瓜

foot *(of person)* jiǎo 脚

✈ 1 foot = 30.5 cm = 0.3 metres

football zúqiú 足球
for gěi 给
  that's for me nà shìr géi wǒ de
forbidden jìnzhǐr 禁止
Forbidden City Zǐjìnchéng 紫禁城
foreign wàiguó 外国
foreign currency wàibì 外币
foreigner wàiguórén 外国人
forest sēnlín 森林
forget wàng 忘
  I've forgotten wǒ wàng le
  don't forget bié wàng le
fork *(to eat with)* chāziR 叉子
form *(document)* biǎo 表
formal zhèngshìr 正式
  (person) zhèngjing 正经
  (dress) lǐfú 礼服
fortnight liǎngge xīngqī 两个星期
forward *(move etc)* xiàng qián 向前
  could you forward my mail? nín néng zhuǎnjì wǒ de xìn ma? 您能转寄我的信吗？
forwarding address zhuǎnjì dìzhǐr 转寄地址
foundation cream féndǐ shuāng 粉底霜
fountain pēnquán 喷泉
fracture gǔzhé 骨折
fragile *(object))* róngyi suì 容易碎
  (health) xūruò 虚弱
France Fǎguó 法国
fraud qīpiàn 欺骗
free zìRyóu 自由
  (no charge) miǎnfèi 免费

c	→ ts
e	→ er
ei	→ ay
ie	→ yeh
iR	→ er
iu	→ yo
o	→ or
ou	→ oh
q	→ ch
ui	→ way
uo	→ war
x	→ sh
z	→ dz
zh	→ j

freight yùnfèi 运费
French (*language*) Fáyǔ 法语
fresh (*fruit*) xīnxian 新鲜
  (*air*) qīngxīn 清新
Friday xīngqī wǔ 星期五
fridge bīngxiāng 冰箱
fried egg zhá jīdàn 炸鸡蛋
fried noodles chǎomiàn 炒面
fried rice chǎofàn 炒饭
friend péngyou 朋友
friendly yóuhǎo 友好
fries shǔtiáo 薯条
from cóng 从
  from England/London cóng Yīnggélán/
  Lúndūn lái
  where is it from? cóng nǎr lái de?
front: in front of you nǐ *qiánmian* 你前面
  at the front zai qiánmian
frost shuāng 霜
frostbite dòngchuāng 冻创
fruit shuíguǒ 水果

> ✈ Some fruit which may be less familiar to
> Westerners:
> **haw** shānzhā 山楂 sourish dark red haw-
> thorn berries, said to be good for the heart
> **kumquat** jīnjú 金桔 small, sharp orange-
> like fruit
> **longan** lóngyǎn 龙眼 juicy white flesh, size
> of an oak-apple, sweet-tasting
> **lychee** lìzhīʀ 荔枝 size of a plum, pink
> bumpy hard skin, white juicy fragrant flesh
> **persimmon** shìziʀ 柿子 soft, orange, sweet-
> tasting fruit

---

fruit salad shuíguǒ shālā 水果沙拉
fry zhá 炸

  nothing fried bú yào zhá de
frying pan jiānguō 煎锅
full mǎnle 满了
  (with food) bǎole 饱了
fun: it's fun hǎowánr 好玩儿
  have fun! hǎohāo wánr 好好玩儿
funny *(strange)* qíguài 奇怪
  (comical) yǒu yìsɪʀ 有意思
furniture jiājù 家具
further gèng yuǎn 更远
fuse bǎoxiǎnsɪʀ 保险丝
future: in the future jiānglái 将来

G

gale dàfēng 大风
gallon jiālún 加仑

> ✈ 1 gallon = 4.55 litres

gallstone dǎnjiéshíʀ 胆结石
gamble dǔbó 赌博

> ✈ Gambling is illlegal apart from in
> Macao and Hong Kong.

garage *(for repairs)* xiūchēchǎng 修车场
  (for petrol) jiāyóu zhàn 加油站
  (for parking) chēkù 车库
garden huāyʋán 花园
garlic suàn 蒜
gas méiqì 煤气
  (petrol) qìyóu 汽油
gay tóngxìngliàn 同性恋
gear *(in car)* dǎng 挡
  (equipment) zhuāngbèi 装备
gents nán cèsuǒ 男厕所
Germany Déguó 德国

c	→ ts
e	→ er
ei	→ ay
ie	→ yeh
ɪʀ	→ yo
iu	→ yo
o	→ or
ou	→ oh
q	→ ch
ui	→ way
uo	→ war
x	→ sh
z	→ dz
zh	→ j

gesture shǒushìʀ 手势

get: will you get me a...? nǐ kéyǐ *géi* wǒ ge...?
你可以给我个 … ?

how do I get to...? wó zěnme néng *dào*...?
我怎么能到 … ?

where do I get a bus for...? wǒ zài nǎr néng *zuò* qù...de gōnggòng qìchē? 我在哪儿能坐去 … 的公共汽车?

when can I get it back? shénme shírhou néng *huán* géi wǒ? 什么时候能还给我?

when do we get back? wǒmen shénme shírhou *huíqù*? 我们什么时候回去?

where do I get off? wǒ zài nǎr *xià chē*? 我在哪儿下车?

have you got...? ní yǒu...ma? 你有 … 吗?

gin dùsōngzǐʀ jiǔ 杜松子酒

gin and tonic jīntānglì 金汤力

ginseng rénshēn 人参

girl nǔháir 女孩儿

girlfriend nǔ péngyou 女朋友

give gěi 给

will you give me...? nǐ néng géi wǒ...ma?

I gave it to him wó gěi tā le

glad gāoxìng 高兴

I'm glad wó hěn gāoxìng

glass bōli 玻璃

(drinking) bōli bēi 玻璃杯

a glass of water yì bēi shuǐ 一杯水

glasses yǎnjìng 眼镜

glue jiāoshuǐ 胶水

glutinous rice nuòmǐ 糯米

go qù 去

I want to go to Shanghai wó xiǎng qù Shànghǎi

when does the bus go? gōnggòng qìchē shénme shírhòu *kāi*? 公共汽车什么时候开?

does this go to the airport? zhè chē qù jīchǎng ma?

the bus has gone gōnggòng qìchē kāi le

he's gone tā *zǒu* le 他 走了

where are you going? nǐ qù nǎr?

let's go wǒmen zǒu ba

go on! jì xù! 继续！

can I have a go? wǒ néng *shìshì* ma? 我能试试吗？

goal défēn 得分

Gobi Desert Gēbìtān 戈壁滩

God shàngdì 上帝

goggles *(for swimming)* yóuyǒng yǎnjìng 游泳眼镜

gold jīnzɪ 金子

golf gāo'ěrfū qiú 高尔夫球

golf course gāoěrfū qiúchǎng 高尔夫球场

good hǎo 好

good! hǎo!

goodbye zàijiàn 再见

got: have you got...? ní yǒu...ma? 你有…吗？

gram kè 克

granddaughter *(son's daughter)* sūnnǚ 孙女
(daughter's daughter) wài sūnnǚ 外孙女

grandfather *(paternal)* yéye 爷爷
(maternal) lǎoye 姥爷

grandmother*(paternal)* nǎinai 奶奶
(maternal) lǎolao 姥姥

grandson *(son's son)* sūnzɪ 孙子
(daughter's son) wài sūn 外孙

grapefruit yòuzɪ 柚子

grapefruit juice yòuzɪ zhī 柚子汁

grapes pútao 葡萄

grass cǎo 草

c	→	ts
e	→	er
ei	→	ay
ie	→	yeh
iʀ	→	er
iu	→	yo
o	→	or
ou	→	oh
q	→	ch
ui	→	way
uo	→	war
x	→	sh
z	→	dz
zh	→	j

grateful: I'm very grateful to you wǒ duì nǐ hěn gǎnjī 我对你很感激

gravy ròuzhī 肉汁

greasy (food) yóunì 油腻
(hair) yóuhūhū 油乎乎

great wěidà 伟大
(very good) hěn hǎo 很好
great! hǎo jí le! 好极了!

Great Hall of the People Rénmín Dàhuìtáng 人民大会堂

Great Wall (of China) (Wànlǐ) Chángchéng (万里)长城

greedy tānxīn 贪心
(for food) chán 馋

green lǜsè 绿色

grey huīsè 灰色

grocer's záhuòdiàn 杂货店

ground dì 地
on the ground zai dì shang
on the ground floor zai yīcéng 在一层

group tuán 团
(at work) xiǎozǔ 小组
our group leader wǒmen de zúzhǎng
I'm with the English group wǒ zài Yīngguó rén de tuán

guarantee bǎoxiū 保修
(assurance) bǎozhèng 保证
is there a guarantee? yǒu bǎoxiū ma?

guest kèren 客人

guide dǎoyóu 导游
(book) zhǐnán 指南

guidebook lǚxíng zhǐnán 旅行指南

guided tour yǒu dǎoyóu de yóulǎn 有导游的游览

guilty yǒuzuì 有罪

guitar jíta 吉他

gum *(in mouth)* yáchuáng 牙床
gun *(pistol)* shǒuqiāng 手枪

H

hair tóufa 头发
  (on body) máo 毛
hairbrush fàshuā 发刷
haircut lǐfà 理发
  where can I get a haircut? wǒ zài nǎr néng lǐfà?
hairdresser's fàláng 发廊
  is there a hairdresser's here? zhèr yǒu fàláng ma?

> ✈ A head and shoulders massage is often included.

hair grip fàqiǎ 发卡
half yíbàn 一半
  a half portion bàn fèn
  half an hour bàn xiǎoshír
  go to **time**
ham huótuǐ 火腿
hamburger hànbǎobāo 汉堡包
hammer chuíʐɪ 锤子
hand shǒu 手
handbag shǒutíbāo 手提包
hand baggage shǒutí xíngli 手提行李
handbrake shǒuzhá 手闸
handkerchief shǒujuàn 手绢
handle *(noun)* bàr 把儿
handmade shǒugōng zuò de 手工做的
handsome yīngjùn 英俊
hanger yījià 衣架
hangover sùzuì 宿醉
  I've got a terrible hangover this

c	→ ts
e	→ er
ei	→ ay
ie	→ yeh
iʀ	→ er
iu	→ yo
o	→ or
ou	→ oh
q	→ ch
ui	→ way
uo	→ war
x	→ sh
z	→ dz
zh	→ j

morning wǒ hē duō le, jīnzǎo hěn *nánshòu* 我喝多了，今早很难受

happen fāshēng 发生

I don't know how it happened wǒ bù zhīrdào zhè shìr zěnme fāshēng le

what's happening? zěnme yàng? 怎么样？

what's happened? fāshēng shénme shìr le?

happy kuàilè 快乐

harbour gángkǒu 港口

hard yìng 硬

(difficult) nán 难

hard-boiled egg zhú lǎo de jīdàn 煮老的鸡蛋

hard seat yìngzuò 硬座

hard sleeper yìngwò 硬卧

harm *(noun)* hàichu 害处

hat màozir 帽子

hate: I hate... wǒ hèn... 我恨…

have yǒu 有

can I have...? néng *gěi* wǒ...ma? 能给我…吗？

can I have some water? wǒ néng *hē* diánr shuǐr ma? 我能喝点儿水吗？

I have no... wǒ méiyǒu...

do you have...? ní yǒu...ma?

I have to leave tomorrow wǒ míngtiān *bìxū* zǒu 我明天必须走

> As with all Chinese verbs, there are no endings. What's more, all of these forms could, depending on context, also mean **I had/I will have** etc
>
> | | |
> |---|---|
> | **I have** wó yǒu | **we have** wǒmen yǒu |
> | **you have** ní yǒu | **you have** nǐmen yǒu |
> | **he/she has** tā yǒu | **they have** tāmen yǒu |

hay fever huāfěnrè 花粉热

he tā 他

> Same pronunciation as for the Chinese for 'she' but a different character.

head tóu 头
headache tóuténg 头疼
headlight chētóu dēng 车头灯
head waiter lǐngbān 领班
head wind nìfēng 逆风
health jiànkāng 健康
  your health! zhù nǐ jiànkāng!
hear: I can't hear wǒ *tīng* bú jiàn 我听不见
hearing aid zhùtīngqì 助听器
heart xīnzàng 心脏
heart attack xīnzàngbìng fāzuò 心脏病发作
heat rè 热
heating nuǎnqì 暖气
heat stroke zhòngshǔ 中暑
heavy zhòng 重
heel jiǎogēn 脚跟
  (of shoe) xiégēn 鞋跟
  could you put new heels on these?
  nín néng géi wǒ huàn xiégēnr ma?
height gāo 高
  (of person) shēngāo 身高
  (of building, mountain) gāodù 高度
hello ní hǎo 你好
  (to get attention) wèi, ní hǎo 喂, 你好
  (on phone) wéi 喂
help bāngzhù 帮助
  can you help me? nǐ néng bāng wǒ ma?
  help! jiùmìng! 救命 !
her[1] tā 她
  I know her wǒ rènshiʀ tā

c	→ ts
e	→ er
ei	→ ay
ie	→ yeh
iʀ	→ er
iu	→ yo
o	→ or
ou	→ oh
q	→ ch
ui	→ way
uo	→ war
x	→ sh
z	→ dz
zh	→ j

> Same pronunciation as for the Chinese for 'him' but a different character.

her² *(possessive)* tā de 她的
  it's her bag zhè shìr tā de bāo

> The de can be omitted when talking about personal relationships.
>
>   **tā fùqin**
>   her father

here zhèr 这儿
  come here dào zhèr lai
hers tā de 她的
hi! hài! 嗨!
high gāo 高
  higher up shàngmian 上面
high chair xiǎohái chīrfàn yòng de gāojiáoyǐ
  小孩吃饭用的高脚椅
hill shān 山
  (on road) pōlù 坡路
  up/down the hill shàng/xià shān 上 / 下 山
him tā 他
  I don't know him wǒ bú rènshir tā
  it's him shìr tā

> Same pronunciation as for the Chinese for 'her' but a different character.

hire *go to* **rent**
his tā de 他的
  his drink tā de yǐnliào
  it's his shìr tā de

> The de can be omitted when talking about personal relationships.
>
>   **tā fùqin**
>   his father

hit: he hit me tā dǎle wǒ 他打了我
hitch-hike dāchē 搭车
hitch-hiker dāchē de rén 搭车的人
hold *(verb)* ná 拿
hole dòng 洞
holiday jiàqī 假期
   (single day) jiàrıʀ 假日
   I'm on holiday wǒ zai fàngjià 我在放假
home jiā 家
   at home zài jiā 在家
   (back in Britain) zài wǒmen nàli
   I want to go home wǒ yào huíjiā
homesick: I'm homesick wó xiǎngjiā 我想家
honest chéngshíʀ 诚实
honestly? zhēnde ma? 真的吗?
honey fēngmì 蜂蜜
honeymoon mìyʊè 蜜月
Hong Kong Xiānggǎng 香港
hope xīwàng 希望
   I hope that... wǒ xīwàng...
   I hope so xīwàng shìʀ zhèiyang
   I hope not xīwàng bú shìʀ zhèiyang
horrible kěpà 可怕
horse mǎ 马
hospital yīyʊàn 医院

c	→ **ts**
e	→ **er**
ei	→ **ay**
ie	→ **yeh**
iʀ	→ **er**
iu	→ **yo**
o	→ **or**
ou	→ **oh**
q	→ **ch**
ui	→ **way**
uo	→ **war**
x	→ **sh**
z	→ **dz**
zh	→ **j**

✈ If you go to hospital, you'll have to register at the Registration Office (挂号处 **guàhào chù**) first and pay a registration fee. You'll have to pay for treatment on the spot, so ask for a receipt.

host zhǔrén 主人
hostess nǔzhǔrén 女主人
hot rè 热
   (spiced) là 辣

I'm so hot! wǒ rè sǐʀ le!

it's so hot today! jīntian zhēn rè!

hotel fàndiàn 饭店

(cheap) lǚguǎn 旅馆

at my hotel zai wǒ zhùde fàndiàn

she is staying at Hotel... tā zhù zài...fàndiàn

> Note that in Chinese you say the name of the hotel before the word for 'hotel'.

> ✈ **lǚguǎn** are more like hostels than hotels; used mainly by Chinese travellers, they are cheap, but guests will usually have to share a room (although Westerners might well be expected to pay more for a single room).

hour xiǎoshíʀ 小时

house fángziʀ 房子

how zěnme 怎么

how many? duōshao? 多少？

how much? duōshao qián? 多少钱？

how much is it? zhè duōshao qián？

how long does it take? yào yòng duōcháng shíʀjiān？要用多长时间？

how long have you been here? nǐ dào zhèʀ duōcháng shíʀjiān le？

how are you? ní hǎo ma？你好吗？

> *YOU MAY THEN HEAR*
> hén hǎo, xièxie *very well thanks*
> hái kéyǐ *so-so*

humid cháorè 潮热

hungry: I'm hungry wǒ è le 我饿了

I'm not hungry wǒ bú è

hurry: I'm in a hurry wǒ yóu diǎn jíshìʀ 我有点急事

please hurry! qǐng kuài diǎnr! 请快点儿!
hurt: it hurts téng 疼
  my leg hurts wó tuǐ téng

husband zhàngfu 丈夫

I

I wǒ 我
  I am English/I am a teacher wǒ shìr Yīngguo
  rén/wǒ shìr lǎoshīr
ice bīng 冰
  with lots of ice jiā hěnduō bīng
ice cream bīngjílíng 冰激凌
iced coffee bīng kāfēi 冰咖啡
identity papers shēnfèn zhèng 身份证
idiot báichīr 白痴
if rúguǒ 如果
ill yǒu bìng 有病
  I feel ill wǒ bù shūfu 我不舒服
illegal bù héfǎ 不合法
illegible bù néng dú 不能读
illness bìng 病
immediately mǎshàng 马上
important zhòngyào 重要
  it's very important hěn zhòngyào
impossible bù kěnéng 不可能
impressive xióngwěi 雄伟
  (person) kuíwǔ 魁梧
improve tígāo 提高
  I want to improve my Chinese wó
  xiǎng tígāo wǒ de Zhōngwén shuǐpíng
in zài 在
  in London zài Lúndūn
  in 1982 zài yī jiǔ bā èr nián
  is he in? tā zài ma?
inch yīngcùn 英寸

c	→ ts
e	→ er
ei	→ ay
ie	→ yeh
iʀ	→ er
iu	→ yo
o	→ or
ou	→ oh
q	→ ch
ui	→ way
uo	→ war
x	→ sh
z	→ dz
zh	→ j

✈ 1 inch = 2.54 cm

include bāohán 包含
  does that include breakfast? bāohán zǎocān ma?
incompetent wúnéng 无能
incredible nányǐ zhìxìn 难以置信
indecent xiàliú 下流
independent dúlì 独立
India Yìndù 印度
Indian (person) Yìndù rén 印度人
indicator (on car) zhǐshìrdēng 指示灯
indigestion xiāohuà bù liáng 消化不良
Indonesia Yìndùníxīyà 印度尼西亚
indoors shìrnèi 室内
infection gánrǎn 感染
infectious chuánrǎn 传染
information zīrliào 资料
  do you have any information in English about...? nǐ yǒu guānyú...de Yīngyǔ zīrliào ma?
  is there an information office? zhèr yǒu wènxùn chù ma? 这儿有问讯处吗?
injection zhùshè 注射
injured shòushāng le 受伤了
injury shāng 伤
innocent wúgū 无辜
  (naive) yòuzhìr 幼稚
insect kūnchóng 昆虫
insect repellent qūchóng jì 驱虫剂
inside zai...li 在…里
insist: I insist wǒ jiānchír yāoqiú 我坚持要求
insomnia shīmián 失眠
instant coffee sùróng kāfēi 速溶咖啡
instant noodles fāngbiànmiàn 方便面
instead dàitì 代替

instead of... ér búshì... 而不是 …
insulating tape juéyuán jiāodài 绝缘胶带
insult wūrǔ 侮辱
insurance bǎoxiǎn 保险
insurance company bǎoxiǎn gōngsīʀ 保险公司
intelligent cōngming 聪明
interesting yǒu yìsiʀ 有意思
international guójì 国际
Internet hùlián wǎng 互联网
Internet café wǎng bā 网吧

> ✈ Internet cafés are widespread, particularly in hotels and university areas. You'll need your passport or an ID card to register.

interpret fānyì 翻译
  would you interpret for us? nǐ kéyi géi wǒmen fānyì yíxià ma?
interpreter fānyì 翻译
into dào... nǐ 到 … 里
  I'm not into that (don't like) wǒ bù xǐhuan nèige 我不喜欢那个
introduce: can I introduce...? wǒ lái jièshào yíxià... 我来介绍一下 …
invalid (disabled) bìng rén 病人
invitation yāoqǐng 邀请
  thanks for the invitation xièxie nínde yāoqǐng
invite: can I invite you out? wǒ néng yuē nǐ chūqu ma? 我能约你出去吗？
Ireland Ài'ěrlán 爱尔兰
Irish Ài'ěrlán 爱尔兰
Irishman Ài'ěrlán nánrén 爱尔兰男人
Irishwoman Ài'ěrlán nǚrén 爱尔兰女人
iron (for clothes) yùndǒu 熨斗
  will you iron these for me? nǐ kéyi bāng wǒ yòn zhèixie yīfu ma?

c	→	ts
e	→	er
ei	→	er
ie	→	yeh
iʀ	→	er
iu	→	yo
o	→	or
ou	→	oh
q	→	ch
ui	→	way
uo	→	war
x	→	sh
z	→	dz
zh	→	j

is *go to* **be**
Islam Yīsīlán jiào 伊斯兰教
island dǎo 岛
it tā 它
  where is it? zai nǎr?

> Chinese does not normally use an
> equivalent for 'it', not being inclined to
> state the obvious.
>
>   **give it to me** géi wǒ *(literally: give me)*
>   **it's not working** bú dòng le *(literally: not
> work)*
>   **I'll take it** wó mǎi le *(literally: I buy)*

Italy Yìdàlì 意大利
itch: it itches yǎngyang 痒痒
itemize: would you itemize it for me? nǐ néng
  měixiàng géi wǒ liè chūlai ma? 你能每项给我
  列出来吗?

J

jacket jiákè 夹克
jade yù 玉
jam guǒjiàng 果酱
  traffic jam jiāotōng dǔsè 交通堵塞
January yīyuè 一月
Japan Rìběn 日本
jaw xiàba 下巴
jealous jídù 嫉妒
jeans niúzǎikù 牛仔裤
jellyfish hǎizhé 海蛰
jetty mǎtóu 码头
jewellery shǒushìr 首饰
job gōngzuò 工作
  just the job zhènghǎo 正好

joke *(noun)* xiàohua 笑话
  you must be joking! nǐ zài kāi wánxiào ba!
  你在开玩笑吧！
journey lǚxíng 旅行
  have a good journey! yílù shùnfēng! 一路顺
  风！
July qīyuè 七月
junction jiāochā lùkǒu 交叉路口
June liùyuè 六月
junk lājī 垃圾
  (food) lājī shípǐn 垃圾食品
  (boat) fānchuán 帆船
just *(only)* jǐnjǐn 仅仅
  (exactly) zhènghǎo 正好
  just a little jiù yìdiǎnr 就一点儿
  just there jiù zài nàr 就在那儿
  not just now xiànzài bùxíng 现在不行
  just now *(at this moment)* xiànzài 现在
  (a short time ago) gāngcái 刚才
  he was here just now tā gāngcái hái zài zhèr
  that's just right zhèngshìr zhèyàng 正是这样

K

Kazakhstan Hāsàkèsītǎn 哈萨克斯坦
kebab kǎo ròuchuàn 烤肉串
keep: can I keep it? wǒ kéyi liúzhe ma?
  我可以留着吗？
  you keep it nǐ liúzhe ba
  keep the change búyòng zhǎo le 不用
  找了
  you didn't keep your promise nǐ
  shíyán le 你食言了
  it keeps on breaking lǎoshìr huài 老是
  坏
key yàoshir 钥匙

c	→ ts
e	→ er
ei	→ ay
ie	→ yeh
iʀ	→ er
iu	→ yo
o	→ or
ou	→ oh
q	→ ch
ui	→ way
uo	→ war
x	→ sh
z	→ dz
zh	→ j

keycard fángjiān kǎ 房间卡
kidney shèn 肾
　　(food) yāozir 腰子
kill shāsǐr 杀死
kilo gōngjīn 公斤

✈ kilos/5 x 11 = pounds

kilos	1	1.5	5	6	7	8	9
pounds	2.2	3.3	11	13.2	15.4	17.6	19.8

✈ When buying food in a market, or ordering fish or dumplings in a restaurant, the Chinese measurements jīn 斤 and liǎng 两 are used. One jīn equals half a kilo, and there are ten liǎng in one jīn.

kilometre gōnglǐ 公里

✈ kilometres/8 x 5 = miles

kilometres	1	5	10	20	50	100
miles		0.62	3.11	6.2	12.4	31	62

kind: that's very kind of you nǐ tài hǎo le 你太好了
　　what kind of...? shénme yàng de...? 什么样的…?
kiosk shòuhuòtíng 售货亭
kiss wěn 吻

✈ Chinese people do not kiss in public, not even when saying goodbye to a loved one.

kitchen chúfáng 厨房
kite fēngzheng 风筝
knee xīgài 膝盖
knife dāo 刀
knock *(verb: at door)* qiāo 敲
know zhīrdào 知道
　　(person, place) rènshir 认识

I don't know wǒ bù zhīrdào
I didn't know wǒ bù zhīrdào
I don't know the area wǒ bú rènshīr zhè yípiàn
Kyrgyzstan Jíěrjísīsītǎn 吉尔吉斯斯坦

L

label biāoqiān 标签
laces xiédài 鞋带
ladies (toilet) nǚ cèsuǒ 女厕所
lady nǚshìr 女士
lager píjiǔ 啤酒
lake hú 湖
lamb (meat) yángròu 羊肉
lamp dēng 灯
lamppost diànxiàngān 电线杆
lampshade dēngzhào 灯罩
land (noun) lùdì 陆地
lane (on road) chēdào 车道
language yǔyán 语言
language course yǔyán kè 语言课
lantern dēnglóng 灯笼
Laos Lǎowō 老挝
laptop bǐjìběn diànnǎo 笔记本电脑
large dà 大
laryngitis hóuyán 喉炎
last zuìhòu 最后
  last year qùnián 去年
  last week/Saturday shàng xīngqī/xīngqī liù 上星期/星期六
  last night zuótian wǎnshang 昨天晚上
  at last! zōngyú dàole! 终于到了!
late wǎn 晚
  sorry I'm late duìbuqǐ wó wǎn le
  it's a bit late yóu diǎn tài wǎn le

c	→	ts
e	→	er
ei	→	ay
ie	→	yeh
iʀ	→	er
iu	→	yo
o	→	or
ou	→	oh
q	→	ch
ui	→	way
uo	→	war
x	→	sh
z	→	dz
zh	→	j

please hurry, I'm late qǐng kuài diǎn, wǒ yào wǎn le

  at the latest zuìwǎn

later hòulái 后来

  see you later huítóujiàn 回头见

laugh *(verb)* xiào 笑

launderette zìrzhù xǐyīfáng 自助洗衣房

lavatory wèishēng jiān 卫生间

law fǎlǜ 法律

lawyer lǜshīr 律师

laxative xièyào 泻药

lazy lǎn 懒

leaf yèzir 叶子

leak lòu 漏

  it leaks zhè dōngxi lòu

learn: I want to learn... wó xiǎng *xué*... 我想学…

lease *(verb)* chūzū 出租

least: not in the least yīdiǎnr yě bù 一点儿也不

  at least zhìrshǎo 至少

leather pízir 皮子

leave *(go away)* zǒu 走

  we're leaving tomorrow wǒmen míngtiān zǒu

  when does the bus leave? gōnggòng qìchē shénme shírhou *kāi*? 公共汽车什么时候开？

  I left two shirts in my room wó bǎ liǎngjiàn chènshān *là* zài fángjiān li le 我把两件衬衫落在房间里了

  can I leave this here? wǒ néng bǎ tā fàng zhèr ma?

left zuǒ 左

  on the left zài zuǒ biān

left-handed zuǒpiězir 左撇子

left luggage (office) xíngli jìcún chù 行李寄

存处

leg tuǐ 腿

legal *(permitted)* héfǎ 合法

lemon níngméng 柠檬

lemonade níngméng sūdáshuǐ 柠檬苏打水

lend: will you lend me your...? nǐ kéyi *jiè* wǒ nǐ de...ma? 你可以借我你的…吗？

lens *(for camera)* jìngtóu 镜头

  (of glasses) jìngpiàn 镜片

less gèng shǎo 更少

  less than that bǐ nà shǎo 比那少

let: let me help ràng wǒ bāng nǐ 让我帮你

  let me go! *(let go of me)* fàngshǒu! 放手！

  will you let me off here? nǐ kéyi ràng wǒ zài zhèr *xiàchē* ma? 你可以让我在这儿下车吗？

  let's go zǒu ba 走吧

  (let's start) kāishǐr ba 开始吧

letter xìn 信

  (of alphabet) zìRmǔ 字母

  are there any letters for me? yóu wǒ de xìn ma?

letterbox xìnxiāng 信箱

lettuce shēngcài 生菜

liable *(responsible)* yǒu zérèn 有责任

library túshūguǎn 图书馆

licence zhírzhào 执照

lid gàir 盖儿

lie *(untruth)* huǎnghuà 谎话

  can he lie down for a bit? tā néng tǎng yìhuǐr ma? 他能躺一会儿吗？

life yíbèiziR 一辈子

  (way of living) shēnghuó 生活

  (living things) shēngmìng 生命

  that's life shēnghuó jiùshìr zhèiyàng!

lifebelt jiùshēng quān 救生圈

lifeboat jiùshēng tǐng 救生艇

c	→	ts
e	→	er
ei	→	ay
ie	→	yeh
iR	→	er
iu	→	yo
o	→	or
ou	→	oh
q	→	ch
ui	→	way
uo	→	war
x	→	sh
z	→	dz
zh	→	j

lifeguard jiùshēng yuán 救生员

life insurance rénshòu báoxiǎn 人寿保险

life jacket jiùshēng yī 救生衣

lift: do you want a lift? nǐ yào *dāchē* ma? 你要搭车吗?

could you give me a lift? néng dā ge chē ma?

the lift isn't working diàntī huài le 电梯坏了

light (not heavy) qīng 轻

(not dark) liàng 亮

the light dēng 灯

the lights aren't working dēng huài le

have you got a light? yóu huǒr ma? 有火儿吗?

light blue qiǎn lánsè 浅蓝色

light bulb dēngpào 灯泡

lighter dáhuǒjī 打火机

like: would you like...? nǐ yào...ma? 你要…吗?

what would you like? nǐ yào shénme?

I'd like a... wǒ yào...

I'd like to... wó xiǎng... 我想…

I like it wó xǐhuan 我喜欢

I like you wó xǐhuan nǐ

I don't like it wǒ bù xǐhuan

what's it like? shénme yàng? 什么样?

do it like this zhèiyàng zuò 这样做

one like that xiàng nà zhǒng 像那种

lime qīng níngméng 青柠檬

lime juice qīng níngméng zhīr 青柠檬汁

line háng 行

(telephone) xiàn 线

lip zuǐchún 嘴唇

lip salve hùchúngāo 护唇膏

lipstick kǒuhóng 口红

list (noun) dānr 单儿

listen tīng 听
  listen! tīng!
litre shēng 升

> ✈ 1 litre = 1.75 pints = 0.22 gals

little xiǎo 小
  a little ice *yìdiǎn* bīng 一点冰
  a little more zài lái yìdiǎn
  just a little jiù yìdiǎn
live zhù 住
  (be alive) huózhe 活着
  I live in… wǒ zhù zai…
  where do you live? nǐ zhù zai nǎr?
liver gān 肝
lizard xīyì 蜥蜴
loaf yìtiáo miànbāo 一条面包
lobster lóngxiā 龙虾
local: could we try a local dish? wǒmen néng
  chángchang *dāngdì de* cài ma? 我们能尝尝当
  地的菜吗?
  a local restaurant dāngdì de fànguǎnr
lock: the lock's broken suǒ huài le 锁
  坏了
  I've locked myself out wó bǎ zìrji suǒ
  zài wàimiàn le
London Lúndūn 伦敦
lonely *(person)* gūdān 孤单
long cháng 长
  we'd like to stay longer wǒmen xiǎng
  zài duō dāi jǐtiān 我们想再多呆几天
  a long time hěn cháng shírjiān
loo: where's the loo? cèsuǒ zài nǎr?
  厕所在哪儿?
look: you look tired nǐ *kàn shàngqù* hěn
  lèi 你看上去很累
  look at that *kàn* a 看啊

c	→ ts
e	→ er
ei	→ ay
ie	→ yeh
iʀ	→ er
iu	→ yo
o	→ or
ou	→ oh
q	→ ch
ui	→ way
uo	→ war
x	→ sh
z	→ dz
zh	→ j

can I have a look? wǒ néng kànkan ma?

I'm just looking wó zhǐʳshìʳ kànkan

will you look after my bags? nǐ néng kān yíxià wǒ de bāo ma?

I'm looking for... wǒ zài zhǎo... 我在找…

look out! dāngxīn! 当心！

loose sōng 松

lorry kǎchē 卡车

lorry driver kǎchē sīʳjī 卡车司机

lose diū 丢

I've lost... wǒ diū le...

excuse me, I'm lost duìbuqǐ, wǒ mílù le 对不起，我迷路了

lost property (office) shīʳwù zhāolǐng chù 失物招领处

lot: a lot hěn duō 很多

not a lot bù hěn duō

a lot of... hěn duō...

a lot more expensive guì hěn duō

lotion rùnfū lù 润肤露

loud (noise) chǎo 吵

(voice) dàshēng 大声

it's too loud shēng tài dà le 声太大了

louder dà diǎn shēng 大点声

lounge (in house) kètīng 客厅

(in hotel) xiūxi shìʳ 休息室

(at airport) hòujīshìʳ 候机室

love: I love you wǒ ài nǐ 我爱你

do you love me? nǐ ài wǒ ma?

he's/she's in love tā zài liàn'ài 他/她在恋爱

I love this beer wǒ ài zhè píjiǔ

lovely kě'ài 可爱

(view etc) hǎo kàn 好看

(meal etc) hǎo chīʳ 好吃

low (wall, hill) ǎi 矮

(price) dī 低

(quality) chà 差
luck yùnqi 运气
 good luck! zhù nǐ hǎo yùn!
lucky zǒuyùn 走运
 you're lucky nǐ zhēn zǒuyùn!
 that's lucky! zhēn zǒuyùn!
luggage xíngli 行李
lunch wǔfàn 午饭
lungs fèi 肺
luxury háohuá 豪华
lychee lìzhīʀ 荔枝

M

Macao Àomén 澳门
mad fēng 疯
made-to-measure dìngzuò 订做
magazine zázhìʀ 杂志
magnificent hǎojí le 好极了
maid *(in hotel)* nǚ fúwùyuán 女服务员
maiden name jiéhūn qián de míngziʀ 结婚前
 的名字

> ✈ Chinese women don't change their
> name when they marry (apart from
> in Hong Kong).

mail xìn 信
 any mail for me? yóu wǒ de xìn méiyou?
mainland dàlù 大陆
main road zhǔ lù 主路
make zuò 做
 will we make it in time? wǒmen *láidejí*
 ma? 我们来得及吗？
make-up huàzhuāng pǐn 化妆品
malaria nüèji 疟疾
malaria tablets yùfáng nüèji de yàopiàn

c	→	ts
e	→	er
ei	→	ay
ie	→	yeh
iʀ	→	er
iu	→	yo
o	→	or
ou	→	oh
q	→	ch
ui	→	way
uo	→	war
x	→	sh
z	→	dz
zh	→	j

预防疟疾的药片

Malaysia Mǎláixīyà 马来西亚

man nánrén 男人

manager jīnglǐ 经理

  can I see the manager? kéyi jiàn jīnglǐ ma?

Mandarin *(language)* pǔtōnghuà 普通话

many hěn duō 很多

  many... hěn duō...

Mao jacket zhōngshānzhuāng 中山装

map dìtú 地图

  a map of Beijing Běijīng dìtú

✈ Bilingual maps are very useful for getting around; showing your destination to a taxi-driver will avoid confusion over places with similar-sounding names.

have you got a bilingual map?
ní yǒu shuāngyǔ dìtú ma?

March sānyuè 三月

market *(in town)* shìchǎng 市场

married jiéhūn le 结婚了

marry: will you marry me? nǐ yuànyì jià géi wǒ ma? 你愿意嫁给我吗？

martial arts wǔshù 武术

marvellous zhēn bàng 真棒

mascara jiémáo gāo 睫毛膏

mashed potatoes tǔdòu ní 土豆泥

massage ànmó 按摩

mat diànzir 垫子

match: a box of matches yì hé huǒchái 一盒火柴

  a football match zúqiú sài 足球赛

material *(cloth)* bùliào 布料

matter: it doesn't matter méi guānxi 没关系

  what's the matter? zěnme le? 怎么了？

mattress chuángdiàn 床垫

mature chéngshú 成熟

maximum zuìdà 最大

May wǔyʊè 五月

may: may I have...? wǒ *kéyǐ* yào...? 我可以要…?

maybe yéxǔ 也许

mayonnaise dànhuáng jiàng 蛋黄酱

me wǒ 我

  he understands me tā liáojiě wǒ

  it's me shìʀ wǒ

  it's for me nà shiʀ wǒ de

meal fàn 饭

mean: what does this mean? zhè shìʀ shénme *yìsi*? 这是什么意思?

measles mázhěn 麻疹

  German measles fēngzhěn 风疹

measurements chǐʀcùn 尺寸

meat ròu 肉

mechanic: is there a mechanic here? zhèʀ yǒu *xiūlǐ gōng* ma? 这儿有修理工吗?

medicine (for cold etc) yào 药

meet pèngjiàn 碰见

  pleased to meet you hěn gāoxìng rènshiʀ nǐ 很高兴认识你

  when shall we meet? wǒmen shénme shírhou *jiànmiàn*? 我们什么时候见面?

  when can we meet again? wǒmen shénme shírhou zài jiàn?

meeting huìyì 会议

melon guā 瓜

member chéngyuán 成员

men nánrén 男人

mend: can you mend this? ní néng *xiū zhèige* ma? 你能修这个吗?

c	→ ts
e	→ er
ei	→ ay
ie	→ yeh
iʀ	→ yeh
iu	→ yo
o	→ or
ou	→ oh
q	→ ch
ui	→ way
uo	→ war
x	→ sh
z	→ dz
zh	→ j

mention: don't mention it búyòng kèqi 不用
客气

menu càidān 菜单
  can I have the menu, please? kàn yíxia
  càidān, xíng ma?

go to pages 77-86

mess yìtuán zāo 一团糟

message liúyán 留言
  (text) duǎnxìn 短信
  any messages for me? yǒu rén géi wǒ liúyán
  ma?
  can I leave a message for...? wó xiáng
  gěi...liúyán

metre mǐ 米

✈ 1 metre = 39.37 inches = 1.09 yds

---

midday zhōngwǔ 中午
  at midday zhōngwǔ

middle zhōngjiān 中间
  in the middle zài zhōngjiān
  in the middle of the road zài mǎlù
  zhōngjiān

midnight bànyè 半夜

might: he might have gone tā kěnéng yǐjing
zǒu le 他可能已经走了

migraine piān tóuténg 偏头疼

mild dàn 淡
  (weather) nuǎnhuo 暖和

mile yīnglǐ 英里

✈ miles/5 x 8 = kilometres

miles	0.5	1	3	5	10	50	100
kilometres	0.8	1.6	4.8	8	16	80	160

---

milk niúnǎi 牛奶

milkshake nǎixī 奶昔

millimetre háomǐ 毫米

凉菜 cold dishes

白斩鸡 **bái zhǎn jī** sliced cold chicken cooked in various herbs

大丰收 **dà fēngshōu** mixed fresh vegetables

夫妻肺片 **fūqī fèipiàn** sliced spicy pig's lung

老醋蛰头 **lǎocù zhétóu** jellyfish in vinegar sauce

凉拌海带丝 **liángbàn hǎidài sīr** shredded seaweed with vinegar

凉拌黄瓜 **liángbàn huángguā** fresh cucumber mixed with finely chopped garlic and vinegar

皮蛋豆腐 **pídàn dòufu** 100 year old eggs with bean curd

小葱拌豆腐 **xiǎocōng bàn dòufu** spring onions mixed with bean curd

素菜 vegetable dishes

菠菜炒鸡蛋 **bōcài chǎo jīdàn** stir-fried spinach with eggs

炒白菜 **chǎo báicài** stir-fried Chinese cabbage

炒豆芽 **chǎo dòuyá** stir-fried bean sprouts

炒土豆丝 **cháo tǔdòusīr** stir-fried shredded potato

醋溜白菜 **cùliū báicài** stir-fried Chinese cabbage in a sour sauce

地三鲜 **dìsānxiān** stewed 'three-fresh' (potato, aubergine and green pepper) vegetables

jǐ wèi?
a table for how many?

nín diǎn shénme?
what would you like to eat?

nín hē diǎn shénme?
what would you like to drink?

c → ts
e → er
ei → ay
ie → yeh
iʀ → er
iu → yo
o → or
ou → oh
q → ch
ui → way
uo → war
x → sh
z → dz
zh → j

I'd like
wǒ yào
我要

蚝油生菜 **háoyóu shēngcài** stir-fried lettuce in oyster sauce

韭菜炒鸡蛋 **jiǔcài chǎo jīdàn** stir-fried Chinese leeks with eggs

烧二冬 **shāo èrdōng** stir-fried mushrooms and bamboo shoots with vegetables

烧茄子 **shāo qiézir** stewed aubergine

松仁玉米 **sōngrén yùmǐ** stir-fried pine nuts with sweetcorn and carrot

素炒西兰花 **sùchǎo xīlánhuā** stir-fried broccoli

西红柿炒鸡蛋 **xīhóngshìr chǎo jīdàn** stir-fried tomato with eggs

西芹百合 **xīqín bǎihé** stir-fried celery with lily root

香菇炒油菜 **xiānggū chǎo yóucài** stir-fried fresh mushrooms and bok choy

鱼香茄子 **yúxiāng qiézir** stir-fried aubergine in hot spicy sauce

豆腐 **bean curd dishes**

家常豆腐 **jiācháng dòufu** home-style bean curd

麻辣豆腐 **málà dòufu** bean curd with chilli and wild pepper

麻婆豆腐 **mápó dòufu** bean curd with minced beef in spicy sauce

三鲜豆腐 **sānxiān dòufu** 'three-fresh' bean curd (made with three ingredients)

沙锅豆腐 **shāguō dòufu** bean curd stewed with mixed vegetables and served as a soup in an earthenware pot

猪肉 pork

叉烧肉 **chāshāo ròu** grilled pork

冬笋肉丝 **dōngsǔn ròusīr** stir-fried shredded pork with bamboo shoots

回锅肉 **huíguō ròu** pork boiled then stir-fried

京酱肉丝 **jīngjiàng ròusīr** stir-fried shredded pork cooked in a sweet black bean paste, served with fresh shredded spring onion

烤乳猪 **káo rǔzhū** roast sucking pig

米粉蒸肉 **mǐfěn zhēngròu** steamed pork with rice

狮子头 **shīzir tóu** large meatball stewed with cabbage

鱼香肉丝 **yúxiāng ròusīr** stir-fried shredded pork in hot sauce

竹筒排骨 **zhútǒng páigǔ** stewed pork chop served in a bamboo tube

禽类 poultry

北京烤鸭 **Běijīng kǎoyā** Peking duck

咖喱鸡 **gālí jī** curried chicken pieces

宫保鸡丁 **gōngbǎo jīdīng** stir-fried diced chicken with peanuts and chilli

怪味鸡 **guài wèi jī** whole chicken with red chilli pepper (strange-tasting chicken)

can I have what he's having? **wǒ kéyǐ hé tā diǎn de yíyàng ma?** 我可以和他点的一样吗？

c	→	ts
e	→	er
ei	→	ay
ie	→	yeh
iʀ	→	er
iu	→	yo
o	→	or
ou	→	oh
q	→	ch
ui	→	way
uo	→	war
x	→	sh
z	→	dz
zh	→	j

酱爆鸡丁 **jiàngbào jīdīng** diced chicken quick-fried with black bean sauce

辣子鸡丁 **làziʀ jīdīng** diced chicken with chilli

麻辣鸡丁 **málà jīdīng** diced chicken with chilli and peppercorns

香酥鸡 **xiāngsū jī** crispy deep-fried whole chicken

香酥鸭 **xiāngsū yā** crispy deep-fried whole duck

牛肉 beef

葱爆牛肉 **cōngbào niúròu** beef quick-fried with spring onions

咖喱牛肉 **gālí niúròu** curried beef

红烧牛肉 **hóngshāo niúròu** beef braised in brown sauce

青椒牛肉 **qīngjiāo niúròu** stir-fried beef with green pepper

铁板牛肉 **tiěbǎn niúròu** Chinese-style beef fajita

羊肉 lamb and mutton

葱爆羊肉 **cōngbào yángròu** mutton quick-fried with spring onions

红烧羊肉 **hóngshāo yángròu** mutton braised in brown sauce

烤羊肉串 **kǎo yángròu chuànr** lamb kebabs

涮羊肉 **shuàn yángròu** Mongolian lamb, served raw, which you dip in a pot of boiling water and eat with a sauce

---

chopsticks
kuàiziʀ
筷子

fork
chāziʀ
叉子

knife
dāo
刀

牙签羊肉 **yáqiān yángròu** shredded spicy roast mutton

孜然羊肉 **zīrrán yángròu** shredded spicy roast mutton with cumin seeds

海鲜 fish and seafood

葱爆海参 **cōngbào hǎishēn** sea cucumber quick-fried with spring onions

干烧桂鱼 **gānshāo guìyú** Chinese perch braised with chilli and black bean sauce

干烧黄鳝 **gānshāo huángshàn** paddyfield eel braised with chilli and black bean sauce

蚝油鲍鱼 **háoyóu bàoyú** stir-fried abalone with oyster sauce

红烧对虾 **hóngshāo duìxiā** prawns braised in sweet and soy sauce

红烧鲤鱼 **hóngshāo lǐyú** carp braised in brown sauce

滑溜鱼片 **huáliū yúpiànr** stir-fried fish slices with thick sauce

清蒸鲈鱼 **qīngzhēng lúyú** steamed bass

糖醋鱼块 **tángcù yúkuàir** sweet and sour fish

虾仁干贝 **xiārén gānbèi** scallops with shrimps

油焖龙虾 **yóumèn lóngxiā** braised lobster

炒鱿鱼丝 **chǎo yóuyú sīr** stir-fried squid slices

water
shuǐ
水

bread
miànbāo
面包

c	→ **ts**
e	→ **er**
ei	→ **ay**
ie	→ **yeh**
iʀ	→ **er**
iu	→ **yo**
o	→ **or**
ou	→ **oh**
q	→ **ch**
ui	→ **way**
uo	→ **war**
x	→ **sh**
z	→ **dz**
zh	→ **j**

蒸螃蟹 **zhēng pángxiè** steamed crab

汤 soups

三鲜汤 **sānxiān tāng** 'three-fresh' soup (prawns, meat and a vegetable)

酸辣汤 **suān là tāng** hot and sour soup

西红柿鸡蛋汤 **xīhóngshìR jīdàn tāng** soup with eggs and tomato

鱼丸汤 **yúwán tāng** fish ball soup

榨菜肉丝汤 **zhàcài ròusīR tāng** soup with shredded pork and pickled mustard greens

紫菜汤 **zǐcài tāng** seaweed soup

米饭 rice

蛋炒饭 **dàn chǎofàn** egg fried rice

米饭 **mǐfàn** rice

扬州炒饭 **yángzhōu chǎofàn** Yangzhou-style fried rice

面食 bread & dumplings

包子 **bāo ziR** steamed buns with various fillings, usually minced pork

葱油饼 **cōngyóubǐng** spring onion pancake

锅贴 **guōtiē** fried Chinese dumplings

花卷 **huājuǎnr** steamed rolls

馄饨 **húntun** dumpling soup

饺子 **jiǎoziR** Chinese dumplings filled with various vegetables and meats

馒头 **mántou** steamed bread

> **more rice please**
> qǐng zài lái diǎn mǐfàn
> 请再来点米饭

烧麦 **shāo mài** steamed Chinese buns, open at the top

水饺 **shuíjiǎo** boiled Chinese dumplings

蒸饺 **zhēngjiǎo** steamed Chinese dumplings

面条 noodles

炒米粉 **chǎo mífěn** fried rice noodles

炒面 **chǎomiàn** fried noodles

担担面 **dàndàn miàn** Sichuan-style noodles in hot sauce

面条 **miàntiáo** noodles

西红柿鸡蛋面 **xīhóngshìʀ jīdàn miàn** noodles in a sauce of stir-fried tomato and eggs

炸酱面 **zhájiàng miàn** cold noodles with black bean sauce and vegetables

甜点 desserts

八宝饭 **bābǎo fàn** eight-treasure (eight varieties of fruit and nuts) rice pudding

冰糖银耳 **bīngtáng yín'ěr** stewed white fungus with lotus-seed and elderberries

果盘 **guǒ pán** mixed fruit

莲子羹 **liánzìʀ gēng** lotus-seed in syrup

酒 wine, spirits etc

二锅头 **èrguōtóu** a common brand of Chinese spirit

very nice!
hén hǎo!
很好！

c → ts
e → er
ei → ay
ie → yeh
iʀ → er
iu → yo
o → or
ou → oh
q → ch
ui → way
uo → war
x → sh
z → dz
zh → j

red wine
hóng
pútaojiǔ
红葡萄酒

white wine
bái pútaojiǔ
白葡萄酒

beer
píjiǔ
啤酒

**bottled
beer**
píngpí
瓶啤

**draught
beer**
zhāpí
扎啤

长城干红 **chángchéng gān hóng**
Great Wall dry red wine

长城干白 **chángchéng gān bái**
Great Wall dry white wine

茅台酒 **Máotái jiǔ** a very famous
and expensive Chinese spirit

米酒 **mǐjiǔ** rice wine

types of preparation

叉烧 **chāshāo** grilled

炒 **chǎo** stir-fried

葱爆 **cōngbào** quick-fried with
spring onions

丁 **dīng** diced

咖喱 **gālí** curried

干烧 **gānshāo** braised with chilli and
black bean sauce

红烧 **hóngshāo** braised in soy sauce

滑溜 **huáliū** stir-fried with sauce

烩 **huì** stewed

火锅 **huǒguō** served with a pot of
boiling water in which you dip the
raw meat, fish or vegetable etc

家常 **jiācháng** home-style (plain)

酱爆 **jiàngbào** quick-fried with black
bean sauce

烤 **kǎo** roast, baked

块 **kuàir** chunks, pieces

片 **piànr** slices

清蒸 **qīngzhēng** steamed

三鲜 **sānxiān** 'three-fresh' (with
three ingredients which vary)

烧 **shāo** braised

什锦 **shíjǐn** assorted
糖醋 **tángcù** sweet and sour
丸 **wán** balls
香酥 **xiāngsū** crispy deep-fried
鱼香 **yúxiāng** stir-fried in hot spicy sauce
炸 **zhá** deep-fried
蒸 **zhēng** steamed
煮 **zhǔ** boiled

meat

狗肉 **gǒuròu** dog
鸡肉 **jīròu** chicken
驴肉 **lǘròu** donkey
牛肉 **niúròu** beef
兔肉 **tùròu** rabbit
鸭 **yā** duck
羊肉 **yángròu** lamb; mutton
猪肉 **zhūròu** pork

vegetables

白萝卜 **bái luóbo** parsnip
白菜 **báicài** Chinese cabbage
扁豆 **biǎndòu** French beans
菠菜 **bōcài** spinach
菜花 **càihuā** cauliflower
冬瓜 **dōngguā** white gourd
豆芽 **dòuyá** bean sprouts
红薯 **hóngshǔ** sweet potato
黄瓜 **huángguā** cucumber
胡萝卜 **húluóbo** carrots
韭菜 **jiǔcài** Chinese leek
卷心菜 **juǎnxīn cài** cabbage

---

orange juice júzirzhīr 桔子汁

mineral water kuàngquánshuǐ 矿泉水

---

c → ts
e → er
ei → ay
ie → yeh
iʀ → er
iu → yo
o → or
ou → oh
q → ch
ui → way
uo → war
x → sh
z → dz
zh → j

蘑菇 **mógu** mushrooms
南瓜 **nánguā** pumpkin
青豆 **qīngdòu** green beans
青椒 **qīngjiāo** green pepper
茄子 **qiéziʀ** aubergine
土豆 **tǔdòu** potato
西红柿 **xīhóngshìʀ** tomato
西兰花 **xīlánhuā** broccoli
心里美 **xīnlíměi** radish
小白菜 **xiǎo báicài** pak-choi
洋葱 **yángcōng** onion
油菜 **yóucài** rape
圆白菜 **yuán báicài** cabbage
竹笋 **zhúsǔn** bamboo shoots

早饭 breakfast

春卷 **chūnjʋǎnʀ** spring rolls
豆浆 **dòujiāng** soybean milk
豆沙包 **dòushābāo** steamed
dumpling with sweet bean paste
filling
火烧 **huǒshao** baked wheaten bun
烧饼 **shāobǐng** sesame pancake
糖火烧 **táng huǒshao** baked
wheaten bun with brown sugar
馅饼 **xiànrbǐng** savoury fritter
油饼 **yóubǐng** deep-fried savoury
pancake
油条 **yóutiáo** unsweetened
doughnut sticks
炸糕 **zhágāo** deep-fried sweet
pancake

the bill,
please
kéyǐ mǎi
dān ma?
可以买
单
吗?

mind: I've changed my mind wó gǎi zhǔyi le
我改主意了
I don't mind wǒ bú jièyì 我不介意
(it's all the same) wǒ wú suǒwèi 我无所谓
do you mind if I...? nǐ jièyì wǒ...ma?
never mind méi guānxi 没关系
mine wǒ de 我的
it's mine shìʀ wǒ de
mineral water kuàngquánshuǐ 矿泉水
minimum zuìxiǎo 最小
minus jiǎn 减
minus 3 degrees língxià sān dù 零下三度
minute fēnzhōng 分钟
in a minute guò yìhuǐʀ 过一会儿
just a minute jiù yì fēnzhōng
mirror jìngziʀ 镜子
Miss xiáojiě 小姐

✈ In Chinese the surname comes first:
Miss Zhou Zhōu xiáojiě.

miss: I miss you wǒ xiáng nǐ 我想你
he's missing tā bújiàn le 他不见了
there is a...missing shǎo le gè... 少了
个...
we missed the bus wǒmen *méi
gǎnshàng* chē 我们没赶上车
mist wù 雾
mistake cuòwu 错误
I think you've made a mistake wǒ
xiáng nǐ fàn le ge cuòwu
misunderstanding wùhuì 误会
mobile (phone) shǒujī 手机
my mobile number is... wǒ de shǒujī
hào shìʀ...
modern xiàndài 现代
moisturizer rùnfū shuāng 润肤霜

c	→ ts
e	→ er
ei	→ ay
ie	→ yeh
iʀ	→ er
iu	→ yo
o	→ or
ou	→ oh
q	→ ch
ui	→ way
uo	→ war
x	→ sh
z	→ dz
zh	→ j

Monday xīngqī yī 星期一
money qián 钱
   I've lost my money wǒ de qián diū le
   I have no money wǒ méi qián

> ✈ The **yuán** 元, the main currency unit of
> China, is usually referred to as the **kuài** 块
> in everyday conversation and when giving
> prices. There are 10 **jiǎo** 角 in one **yuán** 元.
> **Jiǎo** are usually referred to as **máo** 毛.
> There are 10 **fēn** 分 in one **jiǎo** 角.
> Yuán notes come in denominations of 1,
> 2, 5, 10, 20, 50 and 100. There are coins
> for 1, 2 and 5 fēn; 1 and 5 jiǎo; 1 and 2
> yuán. The fēn coins are not very useful.

money belt yāodài qiánbāo 腰带钱包
Mongolia Ménggǔ 蒙古
month yuè 月
moon yuèliang 月亮
moped jīdòng zìxíngchē 机动自行车
more duō yìdiǎn 多一点
   can I have some more? néng zài duō géi wǒ
   yìdiǎn ma?
   more rice, please qǐng zài lái diǎn mǐfàn 请再
   来点米饭
   no more méiyǒu le 没有了
   no more, thanks bú yào le, xièxie 不要了, 谢谢
   more than that bǐ nà duō
   more than... bǐ...duō 比···多
   no more money méi qián le 没钱了
   there aren't any more
   more comfortable gèng shūfu 更舒服

> To make a comparison with 'than' you
> just use the ordinary adjective.
>   **I'm older than her**
>   wó bǐ tā dà *(literally: I than her old)*

morning shàngwu 上午
  good morning ní zǎo! 你早！
  in the morning shàngwu
  this morning jīntian shàngwu
mosque qīngzhēn sìʀ 清真寺
mosquito wénzíʀ 蚊子
mosquito net wénzhàng 蚊帐
most: the most zuì 最
  I like this one the most wǒ zuì xǐhuān zhèige
  most of the people dà duōshù rén 大多数人
mother: my mother wǒ māma 我妈妈
motor mǎdá 马达
motorbike mótuo chē 摩托车
motorcyclist qí mótuo chē de 骑摩托车的
motorist kāichē de 开车的
motor rickshaw diàndòng sānlún chē 电动三轮车
motorway gāosù gōnglù 高速公路
mountain shān 山
  in the mountains zài shān lǐ 在山里

✈ Mountains recognized as tourist sites will always have an entrance gate where tickets are sold for admission. There will generally be concrete steps to the top.

c	→ ts
e	→ er
ei	→ ay
ie	→ yeh
iʀ	→ yeh
iu	→ yo
o	→ or
ou	→ oh
q	→ ch
ui	→ way
uo	→ war
x	→ sh
z	→ dz
zh	→ j

mountaineer dēngshān de 登山的
mountaineering dēngshān 登山
mouse láoshǔ 老鼠
  (for computer) shǔbiāo 鼠标
moustache húzíʀ 胡子
mouth zuǐ 嘴
move: don't move bié dòng 别动
  could you move your car? néng nuó yíxia chē ma? 能挪一下车吗？

movie diànyǐng 电影
Mr xiānsheng 先生
Mrs fūren 夫人
Ms nǚshìʀ 女士

> ✈ In Chinese the surname comes first for all
> these three: **Mr Brown** Bùlǎng
> xiānsheng

much duō 多
　much better hǎo duō le
　not much bù duō
mug: I've been mugged wǒ bèi *qiǎng* le 我被
　抢了
mum: my mum wǒ māma 我妈妈
muscle jīròu 肌肉
museum bówùguǎn 博物馆
mushrooms mógu 蘑菇
music yīnyuè 音乐
must: I must have a... wǒ *bìxū* yào... 我必须
　要...
　I must not eat... wǒ *jué* bù néng chīʀ... 我绝
　不能吃...
　you must do it nǐ bìxū zuò
　must I...? wǒ *yídìng* yào...ma? 我一定要...
　吗？
　you mustn't... nǐ yídìng bùnéng...
mustard jièmo 芥末
my wǒ de 我的

> The **de** can be omitted when talking
> about personal relationships.
>
> 　**wó mǔqin**
> 　my mother

N

nail *(on finger)* zhǐjia 指甲
  (for wood) dīngziʀ 钉子
nail clippers zhǐjiā dāo 指甲刀
nail file zhǐjiā cuò 指甲锉
nail polish zhǐjiā yóu 指甲油
nail scissors zhǐjiā jiǎnziʀ 指甲剪子
naked luótǐ 裸体
name míngziʀ 名字
  my name is... wǒ jiào... 我叫⋯
  what's your name? nǐ jiào shénme míngziʀ?
napkin cānjīn zhǐʀ 餐巾纸
nappy niàobù 尿布
narrow zhǎi 窄
national guójiā 国家
nationality guójí 国籍
natural zìʀ rán 自然
near: is it near? jìn ma? 近吗?
  near here lí zhèr jìn
  do you go near...? nǐ dào...qù ma? 你到⋯去吗?
  where's the nearest...? lí zhèr zuì jìn de...zài nǎr?
nearly chàbuduō 差不多
neat *(drink)* chún 纯
necessary bìyào 必要
  it's not necessary méi bìyào
neck bóziʀ 脖子
  (of dress, shirt) lǐngziʀ 领子
necklace xiàngliàn 项链
need: I need a... wǒ xūyào... 我需要⋯
needle *(for sewing)* zhēn 针
neighbour línjū 邻居
neither: neither of them liǎngge dōu bù
  两个都不

c	→ ts
e	→ er
ei	→ ay
ie	→ yeh
iʀ	→ er
iu	→ yo
o	→ or
ou	→ oh
q	→ ch
ui	→ way
uo	→ war
x	→ sh
z	→ dz
zh	→ j

neither... nor... jì bù...yě bù... 既不···也不···
neither am/do I wó yě bù 我也不
Nepal Níbó'ěr 尼泊尔
nephew: my nephew (brother's son) wǒ zhírzir
我侄子
(sister's son) wǒ wàisheng 我外甥
nervous jǐnzhāng 紧张
net (fishing, sport) wǎng 网
never cónglái 从来
(referring to the future) jué bú huì 决不会
new xīn 新
news xīnwén 新闻
newspaper bàozhǐr 报纸
   do you have any English newspapers? yǒu
   Yīngwén bàozhǐr ma?

> ✈ The English-language *China Daily* is
> available from many hotels and some
> shops.

New Year xīnnián 新年
(Chinese) chūnjié 春节
   Happy New Year! xīnnián kuàilè!
   (Chinese) guònián hǎo! 过年好!

> ✈ Chinese New Year, or Spring Festival, is
> the main festival in China. It usually falls
> between mid-January and mid-February,
> and is a difficult time to travel because
> most people return to their family home.
> **The Lantern Festival** (yuánxiāojié 元宵节)
> marks the end of New Year celebrations.

New Year's Eve xīnnián qiányè 新年前夜
(Chinese) chúxī 除夕
New Zealand Xīnxīlán 新西兰
next xià yíge 下一个
   please stop at the next corner qǐng zài xià

yíge lùkǒu tíng

see you next year míng nián jiàn 明年见

next week/next Tuesday xià xīngqī/ xià
xīngqī èr

next to the hotel fàndiàn *pángbiān* 饭店旁边

next of kin jìnqīn 近亲

nice hǎo 好

(*nice-looking*) hǎo kàn 好看

(*food*) hǎochīr 好吃

niece: my niece (*brother's daughter*) wǒ zhírnǚ
我侄女

(*sister's daughter*) wǒ wàisheng nǚ 我外甥女

night wǎnshang 晚上

good night wǎn ān

at night wǎnshang

night club yèzǒng huì 夜总会

nightdress shuì qón 睡裙

night porter yèjiān zhírbānyuán 夜间值班员

no bù 不

there's no water *méi* shuǐ 没水

I've no money wǒ méi qián

There is no one-word equivalent
to 'no' in Chinese. You can, in an
emergency, use **bù** on its own. But
the natural way of saying 'no' is to
repeat the verb in the question and
put **bù** or **méi** in front of it. (There
is an explanation of the difference
between **bù** and **méi** under 'not').

nǐ lái ma?	bù lái
are you coming?	no (*literally: not come*)

ní yǒu...ma?	méi yǒu
do you have...?	no (*literally: not have*)

c	→ ts
e	→ er
ei	→ ay
ie	→ yeh
iʀ	→ er
iu	→ yo
o	→ or
ou	→ oh
q	→ ch
ui	→ way
uo	→ war
x	→ sh
z	→ dz
zh	→ j

nobody méirén 没人
  nobody saw it méirén kànjian

noisy chǎo 吵
  our room is too noisy wǒmen de fángjiān tài chǎo le

none: none of us speaks Chinese wǒmen *méi yíge rén* shuō Zhōngwén 我们没一个人说中文
  none of them tāmen méi yíge

non-smoker: we're non-smokers wǒmen bù chōuyān 我们不抽烟

noodles miàntiáo 面条

noodle soup tāngmiàn 汤面

nor: nor am/do I wó yě bù 我也不

normal zhèngcháng 正常

north běi 北

Northern Ireland Běi Ài'ěrlán 北爱尔兰

North Korea Běicháoxiǎn 北朝鲜

nose bíziʀ 鼻子

not bù 不
  not that one búshìʀ nèige
  not me búshìʀ wǒ

The main word for 'not' when talking about the present or the future is **bù**.

wó dǒng le I understand	**wǒ bù dǒng** I don't understand
wǒ lèi le I'm tired	**wǒ bú lèi** I'm not tired

If you are using the verb **yǒu** the word for not is **méi**.

wó yǒu shíjiān I've got time	**wǒ méiyou shíʀjiān** I haven't got time

> **yǒu shóuzhǐʀ ma?**
> is there any toilet
> paper?
>
> **méiyǒu shóuzhǐʀ**
> there isn't any
> toilet paper
>
> When you are talking about completed
> events in the past you use **méi** (not **bù**).
>
> **tā méi lái**
> he didn't show up
>
> (If you say **tā bù lái** that would mean 'he's
> not going to show up').
>
> **tā méi gàosu wǒ**
> he didn't tell me
>
> If you want to tell someone not to do
> something, then the word for 'not' is **bié**.
>
> **bié shuō de tài kuài**
> don't speak so fast

note *(bank note)* chāopiào 钞票

nothing: nothing more zài *méi shénme* le 再没
什么了

   nothing for me, thanks wǒ bú yào le,
xièxie 我不要了，谢谢

   there's nothing left yìdiǎn dóu méi
shèng 一点都没剩

November shíʏīyuè 十一月

now xiànzài 现在

nowhere méi dìfang 没地方

nuisance: it's a nuisance zhēn tǎoyàn
真讨厌

   this man's being a nuisance zhè
nánde zhēn tǎoyàn

numb má le 麻了

number *(figure)* shùzìʀ 数字

number plate chēpái 车牌

c	→ ts
e	→ er
ei	→ ay
ie	→ yeh
iʀ	→ er
iu	→ yo
o	→ or
ou	→ oh
q	→ ch
ui	→ way
uo	→ war
x	→ sh
z	→ dz
zh	→ j

nurse hùshɪʀ 护士
nut jiānguǒ 坚果
　(*for bolt*) luósɪʀ 螺丝

O

oar jiǎng 桨
obligatory yǒu yìwù 有义务
obviously míngxiǎn 明显
occasionally óu'ěr 偶尔
o'clock *go to* time
October shíryuè 十月
odd (*number*) dānshù 单数
　(*strange*) qíguài 奇怪
of de 的
　the name of the hotel fàndiàn de míngzɪʀ

> Chinese inverts the order and says *hotel's name*, literally: *hotel of name*.

off: the milk is off niúnǎi *huài* le 牛奶坏了
　it just came off tā gāng *diào* le 它刚掉了
　10% off dá jiǔ *zhé* 打九折

> This means 9/10 of the original price.

office bàngōng shìʀ 办公室
officer (*to policeman*) jǐngguān 警官
official (*noun*) guānyuán 官员
often jīngcháng 经常
　how often? duōjiǔ yícɪʀ? 多久一次？
　how often do the buses go to...? *gé duō cháng shíríjiān yǒu qù...de gōnggòng qìchē?* 隔多长时间有去…的公共汽车？
not often bù jīngcháng 不经常
oil yóu 油
ointment yàogāo 药膏
ok hǎo 好

it's ok *(doesn't matter)* méi guānxi 没关系

are you ok? hái hǎo ma?

that's ok by me wǒ méi wèntí 我没问题

is this ok for the airport? *(bus, train)* qù jīchǎng ma? 去机场吗？

more tea? – no, I'm ok, thanks hái yào chá ma? – búyòng, xièxie 还要茶吗？－不用，谢谢

old *(person)* lǎo 老

　(thing) jiù 旧

how old are you? nǐ duō dà suìshù le? 你多大岁数了？

I am 28 wǒ èrshír bā suì

---

olive gánlǎn 橄榄

omelette jīdàn bǐng 鸡蛋饼

on zài...shàng 在…上

　I haven't got it on me wǒ méi dài 我没带

　on Friday xīngqī wǔ 星期五

　on television zài diànshìr shàng

once *(one time)* yícìr 一次

　(formerly) cóngqián 从前

　at once *(immediately)* mǎshàng 马上

one yī 一

　the red one hóng de 红的

onion yángcōng 洋葱

on-line: to pay on-line zài *wǎng shàng* fù fèi 在网上付费

only zhǐr 只

　the only one zhǐr yǒu yíge

open kāi 开

　I can't open it wǒ kāi bù liǎo zhèige

　when do you open? nǐmen shénme shíhou kāimén? 你们什么时候开门？

open ticket OPEN piào OPEN 票

cʹ	→ **ts**
e	→ **er**
ei	→ **ay**
ie	→ **yeh**
iʀ	→ **er**
iu	→ **yo**
o	→ **or**
ou	→ **oh**
q	→ **ch**
ui	→ **way**
uo	→ **war**
x	→ **sh**
z	→ **dz**
zh	→ **j**

opera gējù 歌剧

operation (surgical) shǒushù 手术

opposite: opposite the hotel fàndiàn duìmiàn 饭店对面

optician's yǎnjìng diàn 眼镜店

or huòzhě 或者

orange (fruit) júzir 桔子

(colour) júhuáng sè 桔黄色

orange juice júzir zhīr 桔子汁

order: could we order now? wǒmen xiànzai néng diǎncài ma? 我们现在能点菜吗？

thank you, we've already ordered xièxie, wǒmen yǐjīng diǎn le

other: the other one lìng yíge 另一个

do you have any others? hái yǒu biéde ma? 还有别的吗？

otherwise yàobùrán 要不然

ought: I ought to... wǒ yīnggāi... 我应该

our wǒmen de 我们的

ours: that's ours nà shìr wǒmen de 那是我们的

out: we're out of petrol wǒmen méiyǒu qìyóu le 我们没有汽油了

get out! chūqù! 出去！

outdoors hùwài 户外

outside: can we sit outside? wǒmen kéyi zuò zài wàimian ma? 我们可以坐在外面吗？

over: over here zai zhèr 在这儿

over there zai nàr

over 40 sìrshír chūtóu 四十出头

it's all over (finished) quán wán le 全完了

overcharge: you've overcharged me nǐ duō shōu wǒ qián le 你多收我钱了

overcooked zuò lǎo le 做老了

overnight (stay, travel) guò yè 过夜

oversleep: I overslept wǒ shuì guò tóu le 我睡过头了

overtake chāoguò 超过
owe: what do I owe you? wǒ qiàn nǐ duōshao?
我欠你多少?
own: my own... wǒ zìrjǐ de... 我自己的…
  I'm on my own jiù wǒ zìrjǐ
owner zhǔrén 主人
oxygen yǎngqì 氧气
oysters mǔlì 牡蛎

P

Pacific Ocean Tàipíngyáng 太平洋
pack: I haven't packed yet wǒ hái méi *dǎ bāo*
  ne 我还没打包呢
package tour tuántǐ lǚyóu 团体旅游
paddy field dàotián 稻田
page *(of book)* yè 页
  could you page him? nǐ kéyi *yòng guǎngbō*
  jiào tā ma? 你可以用广播叫他吗?
pagoda tǎ 塔
pain téng 疼
  I've got a pain in my... wǒ...téng
pain-killers zhǐrténg yào 止疼药
painting *(picture)* huà 画
Pakistan Bājīsīrtǎn 巴基斯坦
Pakistani *(person)* Bājīsīrtǎn rén 巴基斯
  坦人
pale cāngbái 苍白
pancake bǐng 饼
panda xióngmāo 熊猫
panties nèikù 内裤
pants kùzir 裤子
  (underpants) nèikù 内裤
paper zhǐr 纸
  (newspaper) bàozhǐr 报纸
parcel bāoguǒ 包裹

c	→ ts
e	→ er
ei	→ ay
ie	→ yeh
iR	→ er
iu	→ yo
o	→ or
ou	→ oh
q	→ ch
ui	→ way
uo	→ war
x	→ sh
z	→ dz
zh	→ j

pardon? *(didn't understand)* qǐng zài shuō yí biàn 请再说一遍

  I beg your pardon *(sorry)* duìbùqǐ 对不起

parents: my parents wǒ fùmǔ 我父母

park *(garden)* gōngyuán 公园

✈ You usually have to buy a ticket at the gate to enter a public park.

  where can I park my car? wǒ zài nǎr néng *tíng chē?* 我在哪儿能停车？

parking ticket tíngchē fádān 停车罚单

part bùfen 部分

  a (spare) part língjiàn 零件

partner *(boyfriend, girlfriend etc)* liàn rén 恋人

party *(group)* tuántǐ 团体

  (celebration) wǎnhuì 晚会

  I'm with the...party wǒ cānjiā le...tuán 我参加了…团

pass *(in mountain)* guānkǒu 关口

  he's passed out tā yūndǎo le 他晕倒了

passenger chéngkè 乘客

passer-by guòlù rén 过路人

passport hùzhào 护照

past: in the past guòqù 过去

  it's just past the traffic lights guò le hónglǜ dēng jiù shìr 过了红绿灯就是

  go to **time**

> Chinese does not have tenses. Context or another time-related word in the sentence will normally be enough to make it clear when you are talking about the past.
>
> **zuótiān wǒ qù yóuyǒng**
> I went swimming yesterday
> *(literally: yesterday I go swimming)*

But Chinese does have a word **le** to show that an action or event is complete (but not necessarily completed in the past).

wǒ diū le...
I've lost...

wǒ lèi le
I was tired

chē lái le
the bus has arrived,
the bus is here

path xiǎolù 小路
patient: be patient nàixīn diǎn 耐心点
pattern tú'àn 图案
pavement rénxíng dào 人行道
pay fùqián 付钱
  can I pay, please mǎi dān 买单
peace (calm) lěngjìng 冷静
  (not war) hépíng 和平
peach táoziʀ 桃子
peanuts huāshēng 花生
pear lí 梨
peas wāndòu 碗豆
pedal jiǎodēngziʀ 脚登子
pedal rickshaw sānlún chē 三轮车
pedestrian xíngrén 行人
pedestrian crossing rénxíng héngdào
人行横道

✈ Cross with great care. Pedestrians don't always seem to have priority, even at the green man.

peg (for washing) jiāziʀ 夹子
Peking Opera Jīngjù 京剧

c	→ **ts**
e	→ **er**
ei	→ **ay**
ie	→ **yeh**
iʀ	→ **er**
iu	→ **yo**
o	→ **or**
ou	→ **oh**
q	→ **ch**
ui	→ **way**
uo	→ **war**
x	→ **sh**
z	→ **dz**
zh	→ **j**

pen bǐ 笔
  have you got a pen? ní yóu bǐ ma?
pencil qiānbǐ 铅笔
penfriend bíyǒu 笔友
penicillin qīngméi sù 青霉素
penknife qiānbǐ dāo 铅笔刀
pensioner lǐng yánglǎo jīn de rén 领养老金的人
people rén 人
  how many people? duōshao rén?
People's Republic of China Zhōnghuá Rénmín
  Gònghéguó 中华人民共和国
pepper hújiāo 胡椒
  green/red pepper qīng jiāo/hóng shìrzirjiāo
  青椒/红柿子椒
peppermint bòhe táng 薄荷糖
per: per person/night/week měi rén/wǎn/
  xīngqī 每人/晚/星期
per cent: ...per cent bǎifēn zhīr... 百分之···
perfect hǎo jí le 好极了
  the perfect holiday wánměi de jiàqī 完美的假
  期
perfume xiāngshuǐ 香水
perhaps yéxǔ 也许
period (of time) shíqī 时期
  (menstruation) yuèjīng 月经
perm tàngfà 烫发
permit (noun) xǔkě zhèng 许可证
person rén 人
  in person qīnzìr 亲自
personal stereo suí shēn tīng 随身听
petrol qìyóu 汽油
petrol station jiāyóuzhàn 加油站
pharmacy yàofáng 药房

✈ Some pharmacies will help with medical
  problems.

Philippines Fēilǜbīn 菲律宾
phone diànhuà 电话
  I'll phone you wǒ géi nǐ dǎ diànhuà 我给你打
  电话
  I'll phone you back wǒ zài dǎ géi nǐ
  can you phone back in five minutes? nǐ néng
  wǔ fēnzhōng hòu zài dǎ ma?

> **can I speak to...?** wǒ néng gēn…
> shuōhuà ma? 我能跟…说话吗?
> **could you get the number for me?** nǐ
> néng géi wǒ diànhuà hàomǎ ma? 你能给
> 我电话号码吗?

> *YOU MAY HEAR*
> méiyǒu zhège diànhuà hàomǎ
> *this number is no longer in use*
> shìr nǎ wèi? *who's speaking?*
> qǐng shāo děng *hold on*
> qǐng zài dī shēng hòu liúyán *please leave a*
> *message after the tone*

phonebox diànhuà tíng 电话亭
phonecall diànhuà 电话
  can I make a phonecall? wǒ néng dǎ
  ge diànhuà ma?
phonecard diànhuà kǎ 电话卡

> ✈ Almost all phoneboxes take phone-
> cards, such as IC card and IP card.
> You can get these from post offices,
> telecommunication centres (**diànxìn**
> **jú** 电信局) and most newspaper
> stalls.

photograph zhàopiàn 照片
  would you take a photograph of us/

c	→	ts
e	→	er
ei	→	ay
ie	→	yeh
iʀ	→	er
iu	→	yo
o	→	or
ou	→	oh
q	→	ch
ui	→	way
uo	→	war
x	→	sh
z	→	dz
zh	→	j

me? néng bāng wǒmen/wǒ zhàoge xiàng ma?
能帮我们／我照个相吗？

✈ Golden rule: ask permission first if you
want to take someone's photograph.

may I? kéyǐ ma?

piano gāngqín 钢琴
pickpocket páshǒu 扒手
picture huà 画
 (photo) zhàopiàn 照片
piece kuài 块
 a piece of... yí kuài...
pig zhū 猪
pigeon gēzir 鸽子
pill yàopiàn 药片
 are you on the pill? nǐ zài chī *bìyùn yào* ma?
你在吃避孕药吗？
pillow zhěntou 枕头
pin biézhēn 别针
pineapple bōluó 菠萝
pink fěnsè 粉色
pint

✈ 1 pint = 0.57 litres

pipe *(to smoke)* yāndǒu 烟斗
 (for water) shuǐguǎn 水管
pity: it's a pity zhēn kěxī 真可惜
place dìfang 地方
 is this place taken? zhèr yǒu rén ma? 这儿有
人吗？
 do you know any good places to go? nǐ
zhīrdào shénme hǎo dìfang ma?
 at my place zài wǒ jiā 在我家
 at your place zài nǐ jiā 在你家
 to his place dào tā jiā

plain *(noun)* cǎoyuán 草原
  (food) jiǎndān 简单
  (not patterned) sùsè 素色
plane fēijī 飞机
plant zhíwù 植物
plaster *(cast)* shígāo 石膏
  (sticking) chuàngkětiē 创可贴
plastic sùliào 塑料
plastic bag sùliào dài 塑料袋
plate pánzir 盘子
platform *(station)* zhàntái 站台
  which platform please? qǐngwèn, zài jǐhào zhàntái?
play *(verb)* wán 玩
pleasant yúkuài 愉快
please qǐng 请
  could you please...? qǐng nín..., hǎo ma?
  (yes) please hǎo, xièxie 好，谢谢
pleasure kuàilè 快乐
  it's a pleasure bú yòng xiè 不用谢
plenty: plenty of... hěn duō... 很多…
  thank you, that's plenty gòule, xièxie
  够了，谢谢
pliers qiánzir 钳子
plug *(electrical)* chātóu 插头
  (for sink) sāizir 塞子

> ✈ Chinese plugs are both two-pin and three-pin.

plum lǐzir 李子
plumber guǎndào gōng 管道工
plus jiā 加
pm *(1.00 – 6.00)* xiàwu 下午
  (6.00 – 12.00) wǎnshang 晚上
  1pm xiàwu yì diǎn 下午1点
  7pm wǎnshang qī diǎn 晚上7点

c	→ ts
e	→ er
ei	→ ay
ie	→ yeh
iʀ	→ er
iu	→ yo
o	→ or
ou	→ oh
q	→ ch
ui	→ way
uo	→ war
x	→ sh
z	→ dz
zh	→ j

pocket kǒudài 口袋
point: could you point to it? nǐ néng *zhǐ* géi wǒ kàn ma? 你能指给我看吗？
 4 point 6 sìr diǎn liù 4 点 6
police jǐngchá 警察
 get the police jiào jǐngchá 叫警察

✈ Dial 110 for the police. Don't hesitate to ask a policeman for directions.

policeman jǐngchá 警察
police station jǐngchá jú 警察局
policewoman nǚ jǐngchá 女警察
polish (noun) xiéyóu 鞋油
 can you polish my shoes? néng bāng wǒ *cā* xié ma? 能帮我擦鞋吗？
polite yóu lǐmào 有礼貌
polluted wūrǎn le 污染了
pool (swimming) yóuyǒng chír 游泳池
poor: I'm very poor wó hěn qióng 我很穷
 poor quality zhìrliàng *chà* 质量差
pork zhūròu 猪肉
port (harbour) gángkǒu 港口
porter (in hotel) xíngli bānyùn yuán 行李搬运员
portrait xiāoxiàng 肖像
posh (hotel etc) háohuá 豪华
possible kěnéng 可能
 could you possibly...? nǐ néng...ma?
post (mail) xìn 信
postbox (on street) yóutǒng 邮筒
postcard míngxìnpiàn 明信片
poste restante dàilǐng yóujiàn 待领邮件
post office yóujú 邮局

✈ Normally open seven days a week.

potatoes tǔdòu 土豆
pound (weight) bàng 磅

(money) yīngbàng 英镑

✈ pounds/11 x 5 = kilos

pounds	1	3	5	6	7	8	9
kilos	0.45	1.4	2.3	2.7	3.2	3.6	4.1

pour: it's pouring xià dàyǔ ne 下大雨呢

power cut tíngdiàn 停电

power point diànyuán chāzuò 电源插座

prawns dàxiā 大虾

prefer: I prefer this one wǒ gèng xǐhuan zhèige 我更喜欢这个

  I'd prefer to... wǒ gèng yuànyì... 我更愿意…

  I'd prefer a... wǒ gèng xiǎng yào ge... 我更想要个...

pregnant huáiyùn 怀孕

prescription yàofāng 药方

present: at present xiànzài 现在

  here's a present for you zhèshìʀ géi nǐ de *lǐwù* 这是给你的礼物

president *(of country)* zóngtǒng 总统

press: could you press these? nǐ néng bāng wǒ *yùn* zhèixiē yīfu ma? 你能帮我熨这些衣服吗？

pretty piàoliang 漂亮

  pretty good tíng hǎo 挺好

  pretty expensive tǐng guì

price jiàgé 价格

priest shénfù 神父

prison jiānyù 监狱

private sīʀrén 私人

probably kěnéng 可能

problem wèntí 问题

  no problem! méi wèntí!

product chánpǐn 产品

profit lìrùn 利润

promise: do you promise? ní bǎozhèng

c	→ ts
e	→ er
ei	→ ay
ie	→ yeh
iʀ	→ er
iu	→ yo
o	→ or
ou	→ oh
q	→ ch
ui	→ way
uo	→ war
x	→ sh
z	→ dz
zh	→ j

ma? 你保证吗？
I promise wó bǎozhèng
pronounce: how do you pronounce this? zhè zěnme *niàn*? 这怎么念？
properly zhèngdāng 正当
prostitute jìnǚ 妓女
protect bǎohù 保护
protection factor fángshài zhír 防晒值
proud jiāo'ào 骄傲
province shěng 省
public: the public gōngzhòng 公众
public convenience gōnggòng cèsuǒ 公共厕所

> ✈ Most have squat toilets. There probably won't be any toilet paper so best to carry some tissues or paper with you.

public holiday gōnggòng jiàqī 公共假期

> ✈ Public holidays are:
> January 1st, 2nd & 3rd
> Spring Festival (Chinese New Year, one week between mid-Jan and mid-Feb)
> Labour Day (May 1st, one week)
> National Day (October 1st, one week)

pudding bùdīng 布丁
 (dessert) tiándiǎn 甜点
pull *(verb)* lā 拉
pump bèng 泵
puncture dòng 洞
pure chún 纯
purple zǐrsè 紫色
purse qiánbāo 钱包
push *(verb)* tuī 推
pushchair tóng chē 童车
put: where can I put...? wó bǎ...*fàng* zài nǎr?

我把…放在哪儿?
pyjamas shuìyī 睡衣

Q

quality zhìrliàng 质量
quarantine gélí 隔离
quarter sìrfēn zhīr yī 四分之一
  a quarter of an hour yíkè zhōng 一刻钟
  go to **time**
quay mǎtóu 码头
question wèntí 问题

Questions are formed by adding the word
ma to a statement.

tā jiéhūn le	**tā jiéhūn le ma?**
she's married	is she married?
yǒu...	**yǒu...ma?**
there is/are...	is/are there...?

Another way of asking a question is to
repeat the verb or adjective using the
negative **bù** or **méi** (see **not**).

tā máng
he's busy

tā máng bù máng?
is he busy? (*literally: he busy not
busy?*)

tā yǒu piào	**tā yǒu méiyou piào?**
he has the tickets	has he got the tickets?

---

c	→	**ts**
e	→	**er**
ei	→	**ay**
ie	→	**yeh**
iᴿ	→	**yo**
iu	→	**yo**
o	→	**or**
ou	→	**oh**
q	→	**ch**
ui	→	**way**
uo	→	**war**
x	→	**sh**
z	→	**dz**
zh	→	**j**

queue (*noun*) duì 队
quick kuài 快

that was quick zhēn kuài

quiet *(person, street)* ānjìng 安静

  be quiet! ānjìng diǎnr!

quite wánquán 完全

  (fairly) xiāngdāng 相当

  quite a lot xiāngdāng duō

R

radiator *(heater)* nuǎnqì 暖气

radio shōuyīn jī 收音机

rail: by rail zuò huǒchē 坐火车

rain yǔ 雨

  it's raining xiàyǔ ne

raincoat yǔyī 雨衣

rape qiángjiān 强奸

rare xīyǒu 稀有

  (steak) shēng 生

rat láoshǔ 老鼠

rather: I'd rather have a... wǒ hái shìr yào...
我还是要…

  I'd rather sit here wǒ hái shìr zuò zài zhèr ba

  I'd rather not wǒ bú yào

  it's rather hot hěn rè

raw shēng 生

razor *(dry)* guāhú dāo 刮胡刀

  (electric) tìxū dāo 剃须刀

read: something to read néng dú de dōngxi
能读的东西

ready: when will it be ready? shénme shíhou
néng hǎo? 什么时候能好？

  I'm not ready yet wǒ hái méi hǎo ne

real zhēn 真

really zhēn 真

  (very) fēicháng 非常

reasonable *(person)* hélǐ 合理

receipt shōujù 收据
  can I have a receipt please? néng géi wǒ zhāng shōujù ma?
recently zuìjìn 最近
reception (hotel) zǒng tái 总台
  in reception zài zǒng tái
receptionist qiántái 前台
recipe shírpǔ 食谱
recommend: can you recommend...? nǐ néng tuījiàn...ma? 你能推荐···吗？
red hóngsè 红色
reduction (in price) jiǎnjià 减价
red wine hóng pútaojiǔ 红葡萄酒
refuse: I refuse wǒ jùjué 我拒绝
region dìqū 地区
registered: I want to send this registered wǒ yào jì guàhào xìn 我要寄挂号信
relax: I just want to relax wǒ zhír xiǎng fàngsōng yíxia 我只想放松一下
  relax! fàngsōng!
remember: don't you remember? nǐ bú jìde ma? 你不记得吗？
  I don't remember wǒ bú jìde le
rent: can I rent a bicycle? wǒ néng zū liàng zìrxíngchē ma? 我能租辆自行车吗？

c	→ ts
e	→ er
ei	→ ay
ie	→ yeh
iʀ	→ er
iu	→ yo
o	→ or
ou	→ oh
q	→ ch
ui	→ way
uo	→ war
x	→ sh
z	→ dz
zh	→ j

YOU MAY HEAR
duōshao tiān? *for how many days?*
zài...zhīr qián huán huílai *bring it back before...*

➤ Car rental is not possible if you only have a tourist visa (it's not the best way to get around anyhow). You could hire a taxi instead.

rental car zū de chē 租的车

rep dàibiǎo 代表

repair: can you repair it? nǐ kéyi *xiū* ma? 你可以修吗?

repeat: could you repeat that? qǐng nǐ *zài shuō* yíbiàn? 请你再说一遍?

reputation míngsheng 名声

rescue *(verb)* jiù 救

reservation yùdìng 预订

  I want to make a reservation for... wó xiǎng yùdìng... 我想预订…

reserve: can I reserve a seat? wǒ néng *dìng* ge wèizir ma? 我能订个位子吗?

> *YOU MAY THEN HEAR*
> jí diǎn? *for what time?*
> nín de xìngmíng? *and your name is?*

residence permit jūliúzhèng 居留证

responsible fù zé 负责

rest: I've come here for a rest wǒ dào zhèr lái *xiūxi* 我到这儿来休息

  you keep the rest shèngxià de géi nǐ 剩下的给你

restaurant fànguǎn 饭馆

> ✈ If you're in a group of Chinese people, it's usual for one person to pay the bill for the entire party. Trying to pay your share may cause embarrassment, so it's best to reciprocate by paying the whole bill at the next meal. Many Chinese restaurants have fish tanks from which diners can select the fish they want for dinner. Live turtles, crayfish and frogs are also a common sight in restaurants.

restaurant car cānchē 餐车

retired tuìxiū le 退休了

return: a return to... qù...de wángfǎn piào 去…的往返票

> ✈ You can get a return flight within China, but on the railways there are only single tickets.

reverse charge call duìfāng fùfèi diànhuà 对方付费电话

reverse gear dàochē dǎng 倒车档

rheumatism fēngshīɪ 风湿

rib lèigǔ 肋骨

rice dàmǐ 大米

  (cooked) mǐfàn 米饭

> ✈ In a formal meal, rice is often served after the main dishes, and is regarded as a filler.

rice noodles mǐfěn 米粉

rice wine mǐjiǔ 米酒

rich *(person)* yǒuqián 有钱

rickshaw rénlìchē 人力车

ridiculous kěxiào 可笑

right: that's right duì le 对了

  you're right nǐ duì le

  on the right zài yòubiān 在右边

  right! *(understood)* hǎo de! 好的！

ring *(on finger)* jièzhiɪ 戒指

ripe shú 熟

rip-off: it's a rip-off zhè shìɪ qiāo zhúgàng 这是敲竹杠

river hé 河

  (big) jiāng 江

RMB rénmínbì 人民币

road lù 路

  which is the road to...? něi tiáo shìɪ qù...de lù?

c	→ ts
e	→ er
ei	→ ay
ie	→ yeh
iɪ	→ yo
iu	→ yo
o	→ or
ou	→ oh
q	→ ch
ui	→ way
uo	→ war
x	→ sh
z	→ dz
zh	→ j

road map jiāotōng tú 交通图

rob: I've been robbed wǒ bèi *qiǎng* le 我被抢了

rock yánshír 岩石

roll *(bread)* miànbāo 面包

romantic làngmàn 浪漫

roof fángdǐng 房顶

room fángjiān 房间

have you got a single/double room? nǐmen yǒu dān/shuāng rén jiān ma?

> YOU MAY THEN HEAR
> duìbuqǐ, wǒmen kè mǎn le *sorry, we're full*
> yào bú yào yùpén? *with or without bath?*
> zhù jí wǎn? *for how many nights?*

> for one night yì wǎn 一晚
> for three nights sān wǎn

room service kèfáng fúwù 客房服务

rope shéngzir 绳子

rose méiguī 玫瑰

rough *(sea)* fēnglàng hěn dà 风浪很大

roughly *(approx)* dàyuē 大约

round *(circular)* yuán 圆

it's my round gāi wó mǎi le 该我买了

roundabout *(on road)* huán dǎo 环岛

route lùxiàn 路线

rowing boat shǒu huá chuán 手划船

rubber *(material)* xiàngjiāo 橡胶

(eraser) xiàngpí 橡皮

rubber band xiàngpí jīnr 橡皮筋儿

rubbish *(waste)* lājī 垃圾

(poor quality goods) lièzhìr pǐn 劣质品

rubbish! húshuō! 胡说！

rucksack bēibāo 背包

rude cūlǔ 粗鲁

ruin fèixū 废墟
rum lángmú jiǔ 朗姆酒
  a rum and coke lángmújiǔ jiā kělè
run: hurry, run! kuài, pǎo! 快，跑！
  I've run out of petrol/money wǒ méi qìyóu/
  qián le 我没汽油/钱了
Russia Éguó 俄国

S

sad nánguò 难过
  (situation) zāo 糟
safe ānquán 安全
  will it be safe here? zhèr ānquán ma?
  is it safe to swim here? zài zhèr yóuyǒng
  ānquán ma?
safety ānquán 安全
safety pin biézhēn 别针
sailor shuíshǒu 水手
salad shālā 沙拉
sale: is it for sale? zhè mài ma? 这卖吗？
salmon sānwén yú 三文鱼
salt yán 盐
same yíyàng 一样
  the same again, please zài lái yíge
  再来一个
  it's all the same to me wǒ wú suǒwèi
  我无所谓
sand shāziʀ 沙子
sandals liángxié 凉鞋
sandwich sānmíngzhìʀ 三明治
  a ham/cheese sandwich huótuǐ/nǎilào
  sānmíngzhìʀ
sanitary towels wèishēng jīn 卫生巾
satisfactory ràng rén mǎnyì 让人满意
Saturday xīngqī liù 星期六

c	→	ts
e	→	er
ei	→	ay
ie	→	yeh
iʀ	→	er
iu	→	yo
o	→	or
ou	→	oh
q	→	ch
ui	→	way
uo	→	war
x	→	sh
z	→	dz
zh	→	j

sauce tāngzhīr 汤汁
saucepan píngdǐ guō 平底锅
saucer diézir 碟子
sauna sāngná 桑拿
sausage xiāngcháng 香肠
say shuō 说
  how do you say...in Chinese? Zhōngwén...
  zěnme shuō? 中文 … 怎么说?
  what did he say? tā shuō shénme?
scarf wéijīn 围巾
  (for head) tóujīn 头巾
scenery fēngjǐng 风景
schedule rìrchéng 日程
  (programme) shírkè biǎo 时刻表
  on schedule zhǔnshír 准时
  behind schedule wándiǎn 晚点
scheduled flight bānjī 班机
school xuéxiào 学校
scissors: a pair of scissors yìbá jiǎnzir 一把剪子
scooter *(motorized)* xiǎo mótuō chē 小摩托车
Scotland Sūgélán 苏格兰
Scottish Sūgélán 苏格兰
scream jiānjiào 尖叫
screw *(noun)* luósīr dīng 螺丝钉
screwdriver luósīr dāo 螺丝刀
sea hǎi 海
  by the sea zài hǎi biān 在海边
seafood hǎixiān 海鲜
search *(verb)* zhǎo 找
search party sōusuǒ duì 搜索队
seasick: I get seasick wǒ yūnchuán 我晕船
seaside hǎi biān 海边
  let's go to the seaside wǒmen qù hǎibiān
  ba?
season jìjié 季节
  the high/low season wàngjì/dànjì 旺季 /

淡季

seasoning zuǒliào 佐料

seat zuòwèi 座位

is this somebody's seat? zhèige zuòwei yǒu rén ma?

seatbelt ānquán dài 安全带

> ✈ Seatbelts are rarely worn in China. So when getting into a taxi, remember to wipe the dirt off the seat belt to avoid staining your clothes!

seaweed hǎidài 海带

second (adjective) dì'èr 第二

(of time) miǎo 秒

the second of... (date) ...èr hào ···二号

secondhand èrshǒu 二手

see kànjian 看见

have you seen...? nǐ kànjian...le ma?

can I see the room? wǒ néng kànkan zhèige fángjiān ma? 我能看看这个房间吗？

see you! zàijiàn! 再见！

see you tonight wǎnshang jiàn! 晚上见！

oh, I see è, wǒ míngbai le 哦，我明白了

self-service zìrzhù 自助

sell mài 卖

send jì 寄

I want to send this to England wǒ yào bǎ zhèige jì dào Yīngguó

sensitive mín'gǎn 敏感

separate (adjective) fēnkai 分开

I'm separated wǒ fēnjǔ le 我分居了

separately: can we pay separately? wǒmen néng fēnkāi fù ma? 我们能分开付吗？

c	→ ts
e	→ er
ei	→ ay
ie	→ yeh
iʀ	→ er
iu	→ yo
o	→ or
ou	→ oh
q	→ ch
ui	→ way
uo	→ war
x	→ sh
z	→ dz
zh	→ j

September jiǔyuè 九月
serious *(person)* yánsù 严肃
  (situation, illness) yánzhòng 严重
  I'm serious wǒ shìʀ rènzhēn de 我是认真的
  this is serious zhè hěn yánzhòng
  is it serious, doctor? yīsheng, zhè yánzhòng ma?
service: is service included? bāokuò *fúwù* ma? 包括服务吗？
service station jiāyóu zhàn 加油站
serviette cānjīn 餐巾
several jǐge 几个
sex *(act)* xìngjiāo 性交
  (gender) xìngbié 性别
sexy xìnggǎn 性感
shade: in the shade zài yīnliángr 在阴凉儿
shake yáo 摇
  to shake hands wò shǒu 握手

> ✈ Chinese shake hands as Westerners do, particularly among men. If meeting an older or senior person, it's best to leave the initiative to them. There is also the traditional Chinese gesture of cupping one hand in the other in front of the chest.

shallow qiǎn 浅
shame: what a shame! zhēn kěxī! 真可惜！
shampoo xǐfà shuǐ 洗发水
share fèn 份
  (room, table) héyòng 合用
shark shāyú 鲨鱼
sharp kuài 快
  (taste) zhēn suān 真酸
  (pain) jùliè 剧烈
shave tì 剃
shaver diàn tì dāo 电剃刀

shaving foam tìxū pàomò 剃须泡沫
shaving point diàntìdāo chāxiāo 电剃刀插销
she tā 她

> Same pronunciation as for the Chinese for
> 'he' but a different character.

sheet chuángdān 床单
shelf jiàziʀ 架子
shell (sea-) ké 壳
shellfish bèilèi 贝类
shelter bì 蔽
  can we shelter here? wǒmen néng zài zhèr
  bìbì ma?
sherry xuělì jiǔ 雪利酒
ship chuán 船
shirt chènshān 衬衫
shit! zāole! 糟了!
shock chīrjīng 吃惊
  I got an electric shock from the... wǒ
  bèi...diàn le yíxia 我被⋯电了一下
shoelaces xiédài 鞋带
shoes xié 鞋

> ✈ In most private houses, shoes are
> left at the front door and slippers
> are worn inside.

> ✈ men: 40 41 42 43 44 45
> women: 36 37 38 39 40 41
> UK: 3   4   5   6   7   8 9 10 11
>
> China uses the continental sizing
> system.

shop shāngdiàn 商店
  I've some shopping to do wǒ yào mǎi
  dōngxi 我要买东西

c	→ ts
e	→ er
ei	→ ay
ie	→ yeh
iʀ	→ er
iu	→ yo
o	→ or
ou	→ oh
q	→ ch
ui	→ way
uo	→ war
x	→ sh
z	→ dz
zh	→ j

✈ Haggling for goods is very much the norm in markets – but remember that it is *not* done in restaurants and shops. Shops are usually open until at least eight o'clock at night. In many department stores you must get a ticket for your purchases at one desk before paying the cashier at another desk. You then collect your purchases from where you got the ticket.

shop assistant shòuhuò yʋán 售货员
short duǎn 短
  (person) ǎi 矮
short cut jiéjìng 捷径
shorts duǎnkù 短裤
shoulder jiānbǎng 肩膀
shout hǎn 喊
show: please show me qǐng ràng wǒ *kànkan* 请让我看看
shower: with shower dài *línyù* de 带淋浴的
shrimps xiǎo xiā 小虾
shut guān 关
  they're shut guānmén le 关门了
  when do you shut? nǐmen jídiǎn guānmén?
  shut up! bì zuǐ! 闭嘴！
shy hàixiū 害羞
sick bìng 病
  (nauseous) ěxin 恶心
  I feel sick wó xiǎng tù 我想吐
  he's been sick tā tù le 他吐了
side biān 边
  by the side of the road zài lùbiān
side street hútòng 胡同
sight: the sights of... ...de míngshèng …的名胜
sightseeing tour yóulǎn 游览

sign *(notice)* páizіʀ 牌子
  (road sign) lùbiāo 路标
signal: he didn't signal tā méi dǎ xìnhào 他没
打信号
signature qiānzìʀ 签字
silence jìng 静
  (of person) chénmò 沉默
silk sīʀchóu 丝绸
silly *(person)* bèn 笨
  (thing to do) chǔn 蠢
silver yín 银
similar xiāngsìʀ 相似
simple jiǎndān 简单
since: since last week zìʀcóng shàngge xīngqī
自从上个星期
  since we arrived zìʀcóng wǒmen dào zhèr
  (because) yīnwèi 因为
sincere zhēnchéng 真诚
sing chàng 唱
Singapore Xīnjiāpō 新加坡
single: I'm single wǒ shìʀ dānshēn 我是单身
  a single to... yìzhāng qù...de *dānchéng
piào* 一张去…的单程票
single room dān jiān 单间
sister: my sister *(older)* wǒ jiějie 我姐姐
  (younger) wǒ mèimei 我妹妹
sit: can I sit here? wǒ kéyi *zuò* zhèr ma?
我可以坐这儿吗？
size hào 号
skates bīngxié 冰鞋
skating rink huábīng chǎng 滑冰场
ski *(noun)* huáxuě bǎn 滑雪板
  (verb) huáxuě 滑雪
ski boots huáxuě xié 滑雪鞋
skiing huáxuě 滑雪
ski lift suǒdào 索道

c	→ ts
e	→ er
ei	→ ay
ie	→ yeh
iʀ	→ er
iu	→ yo
o	→ or
ou	→ oh
q	→ ch
ui	→ way
uo	→ war
x	→ sh
z	→ dz
zh	→ j

skin pífū 皮肤

skin-diving qiánshuǐ 潜水

skirt qúnzir 裙子

sky tiānkōng 天空

sledge xuěqiāo 雪撬

sleep: I can't sleep wǒ *shuì* bù zháo 我睡不着

sleeper *(rail)* wòpù 卧铺

sleeping bag shuìdài 睡袋

sleeping pill ānmiányào 安眠药

sleeve xiùzir 袖子

slide *(photo)* huàndēng piān 幻灯片

slow màn 慢

  could you speak a little slower? nǐ néng shuō màn diǎnr ma?

slowly màn 慢

small xiǎo 小

  smaller notes gèng xiǎo de língqián 更小的
  零钱

small change língqián 零钱

smallpox tiānhuā 天花

smell: there's a funny smell yǒu guài *wèir* 有怪味儿

  it smells yǒu wèir

smile *(verb)* xiào 笑

smoke *(noun)* yān 烟

  do you smoke? nǐ chōu yān ma? 你抽烟吗?

  may I smoke? wǒ néng chōu yān ma?

snack xiǎochīr 小吃

snake shé 蛇

snow xuě 雪

  it's snowing xià xuě le

so: it's so hot today jīntiān *tài* rè le 今天太热了

  not so much méi nàme duō 没那么多

  so am/do I wó yě shìr 我也是

soap xiāngzào 香皂

soap powder xǐyī fěn 洗衣粉

sober qīngxǐng 清醒
socks wàziʀ 袜子
soda (water) sūdá 苏打
soft drink ruán yǐnliào 软饮料
soft seat ruǎnzuò 软座
soft sleeper ruǎnwò 软卧
software ruǎn jiàn 软件
sole xiédǐ 鞋底
some: some people yīxiē rén 一些人
  some beer yīxiē píjiǔ
  some crisps yīxiē shǔpiànr
  can I have some? wǒ néng lái *diǎnr* ma? 我能来点儿吗？
  can I have some bread? wǒ néng yào diǎnr miànbāo ma?
somebody yǒurén 有人
something mǒu wù 某物
sometimes yǒu shíʀhou 有时侯
somewhere mǒu dì 某地
son: my son wǒ érziʀ 我儿子
song gē 歌
soon yìhuǐ 一会儿
  as soon as possible yuè kuài yuè hǎo 越快越好
  sooner gèng kuài 更快
sore: it's sore téng 疼
  sore throat sǎngziʀ téng 嗓子疼
sorry: (I'm) sorry duìbuqǐ 对不起
  sorry? nǐ shuō shénme? 你说什么？
sort: this sort zhèiyàng de 这样的
  what sort of...? shénme yàng de...?
  will you sort it out? nǐ néng *jiějué* zhè shìʀ ma? 你能解决这事吗？
so-so hái kéyǐ 还可以
soup tāng 汤
sour suān 酸

c	→	ts
e	→	er
ei	→	ay
ie	→	yeh
iʀ	→	er
iu	→	yo
o	→	or
ou	→	oh
q	→	ch
ui	→	way
uo	→	war
x	→	sh
z	→	dz
zh	→	j

south nán 南
South Africa Nánfēi 南非
South China Sea Nánhǎi 南海
South Korea Nánhán 南韩
souvenir jìniàn pǐn 纪念品
soya milk dòujiāng 豆浆
soy sauce jiàngyóu 酱油
spade tiěqiāo 铁锹
Spain Xībānyá 西班牙
spanner bānshǒu 扳手
speak shuō 说
  do you speak English? nǐ shuō Yīngyǔ ma?
  I don't speak Chinese wǒ bù shuō Zhōngwén
special tèbié 特别
specialist zhuānjiā 专家
spectacles yǎnjīng 眼镜
speed sùdu 速度
  he was speeding tā chāosù le 他超速了
speed limit sùdu xiànzhì 速度限制
spend (money) huā 花
spice zuǒliào 佐料
  is it spicy? zhè là ma? 这辣吗?
spider zhīrzhū 蜘蛛
spoon sháozir 勺子
sprain: I've sprained my... wǒ de...niǔ le 我的
  …扭了
spring (of car, seat) tánhuáng 弹簧
  (season) chūntiān 春天
square (in town) guángchǎng 广场
  two square metres liǎng píngfāng mǐ 2 平方
  米
stairs lóutī 楼梯
stalls xiǎo tānr 小摊儿
stamp yóupiào 邮票
  two stamps for England jì liǎng fēng Yīngguó
  xìn de yóupiào

stand *(verb)* zhàn 站
stand-by: to fly stand-by zài děnghòu míngdān shàng 在等候名单上
star xīngxing 星星
start: when does it start? shénme shíⱨou kāishǐ? 什么时候开始?
  my car won't start wǒ de chē qǐdòng bù liǎo 我的车起动不了
starving: I'm starving wǒ è jí le 我饿极了
station chēzhàn 车站
statue sùxiàng 塑像
stay zhù 住
  we enjoyed our stay wǒmen zhù de hěn gāoxìng
  stay there dāi zài nàr 呆在那儿
  I'm staying at... wǒ zhù zài...
steak niúpái 牛排

well done quán shóu
medium bàn shóu
rare shēng de

steal: my wallet's been stolen wǒ de qiánbāo bèi tōu le 我的钱包被偷了
steamed bread mántou 馒头

> ✈ Try this as a snack from a street stall.

steep dǒu 陡
step *(of stairs)* táijiē 台阶
sterling yīngbàng 英镑
stewardess kōngzhōng xiáojiě 空中小姐
sticking plaster chuàng kě tiē 创可贴
sticky nián 黏
sticky rice nuòmǐ 糯米
stiff yìng 硬
still: keep still bié dòng! 别动!
  I'm still here wǒ hái zài 我还在

c	→	ts
e	→	er
ei	→	ay
ie	→	yeh
iʀ	→	er
iu	→	yo
o	→	or
ou	→	oh
q	→	ch
ui	→	way
uo	→	war
x	→	sh
z	→	dz
zh	→	j

I'm still waiting wǒ hái zài děng

sting: I've been stung wó bèi zhē le 我被蛰了

stink (noun) chòuwèi 臭味

　it stinks zhēn chòu 真臭

stir-fry chǎo 炒

stomach wèi 胃

　have you got something for an upset stomach? yǒu shénme zhìr wèi bù hǎo de yào ma?

stomach-ache: I have a stomach-ache wǒ wèiténg 我胃疼

stone shíRtou 石头

✈ 1 stone = 6.35 kilos

stop (for buses) chēzhàn 车站

　stop! tíng! 停！

　do you stop near...? zài...tíng ma?

　could you stop here? nǐ néng zài zhèr tíng ma?

stop-over zhōngtú tíngliú 中途停留

　can we make a stop-over in Suzhou? wǒmen néng zài Sūzhōu tíng yíxià ma? 我们能在苏州停一下吗?

storm bàofēng yǔ 暴风雨

straight zhíR 直

　go straight on zhíR zǒu

　a straight whisky bù jiā shuǐ de wēishìRjì 不加水的威士忌

straightaway mǎshàng 马上

strange (odd) qíguài 奇怪

　(unknown) mòshēng 陌生

stranger shēngrén 生人

　I'm a stranger here wǒ dìyīcìR lái zhèr 我第一次来这儿

strawberry cǎoméi 草莓

street jiē 街

street map jiēqū tú 街区图
string: have you got any string? ní yǒu *xìshéng* ma? 你有细绳吗？
stroke: he's had a stroke tā zhòngfēng le 他中风了
strong zhuàng 壮
  (drink) liè 烈
stuck *(drawer etc)* qiǎ zhù le 卡住了
student xuésheng 学生
stupid shǎ 傻
subtitles fù biāo tí 副标题
such: such a lot zhème duō 这么多
suddenly tūrán 突然
sugar táng 糖
suit *(man's)* xīfú 西服
suitable héshìʀ 合适
suitcase shǒutí xiāng 手提箱
summer xiàtian 夏天
sun tàiyang 太阳
  in the sun zài tàiyang dǐxia
  out of the sun bú zài tàiyang dǐxia
sunbathe rìʀguāng yù 日光浴
sun block fángshài shuāng 防晒霜
sunburn shài shāng 晒伤
sun cream fángshài shuāng 防晒霜
Sunday xīngqī tiān 星期天
sunglasses tàiyang jìng 太阳镜
sun lounger tàiyang yǐ 太阳椅
sunstroke zhòngshǔ 中暑
suntan shài hēi 晒黑
suntan oil rìʀguāng yù yóu 日光浴油
supermarket chāo shìʀ 超市

c	→ **ts**
e	→ **er**
ei	→ **ay**
ie	→ **yeh**
iʀ	→ **er**
iu	→ **yo**
o	→ **or**
ou	→ **oh**
q	→ **ch**
ui	→ **way**
uo	→ **war**
x	→ **sh**
z	→ **dz**
zh	→ **j**

✈ If you have a bag with you when you enter a supermarket, you'll generally have to leave it with an attendant, who'll give you a numbered token to wear on your wrist until you've finished shopping.

supper wǎnfàn 晚饭

sure: I'm not sure wǒ bùnéng kěndìng 我不能肯定

are you sure? ní kěndìng ma?

sure! dāngrán! 当然！

surfboard chōnglàng bǎn 冲浪板

surfing: to go surfing qù chōnglàng 去冲浪

surname xìng 姓

> ✈ Chinese surnames precede given names. In the name **Wáng Huá** 王华, **Wáng** 王 is the surname and **Huá** 华 the given name.

swearword zāng huà 脏话

sweat (verb) chūhàn 出汗

sweater máoyī 毛衣

sweet (dessert) tiándiǎn 甜点

(wine) tián 甜

it's too sweet tài tián le

sweet and sour tángcù 糖醋

sweets táng 糖

swerve: I had to swerve wó zhǐʀ néng jízhuǎnwān 我只能急转弯

swim: I'm going for a swim wǒ qù yóuyǒng 我去游泳

I can't swim wǒ bú huì yóuyǒng

let's go for a swim zánmen qù yóuyǒng

swimming costume yóuyǒng yī 游泳衣

swimming pool yóuyǒng chíʀ 游泳池

> ✈ Swimming caps are often required in Chinese swimming pools. You can usually hire or buy one at the pool.

I'd like a swimming cap please qǐng géi wǒ ge yǒngmào

switch kāiguān 开关
  to switch on kāi 开
  to switch off guān 关

T

table zhuōzir 桌子
  a table for four yì zhāng sìr ge rén de zhuōzir
table tennis pīngpāngqiú 乒乓球
Tajikistan Tǎjíkèsītǎn 塔吉克斯坦
take ná 拿
  can I take this (with me)? kéyi ná ma?
  will you take me to the airport? néng sòng wǒ qù jīchǎng ma? 能送我去机场吗?
  how long will it take? yào duōcháng shírjiān? 要多长时间?
  somebody has taken my bags yǒu rén ná le wǒ de bāo
  can I take you out tonight? jīnwǎn wǒ kéyi qǐng nǐ chūqu ma? 今晚我可以请你出去吗?
  is this seat taken? zhèr yǒu rén ma? 这儿有人吗?
  I'll take it wǒ yào le 我要了
talk (verb) shuōhuà 说话
tall gāo 高
tampons wèishēng shuān 卫生栓
tan (from sun) shài hēi 晒黑
tank (of car) yóuxiāng 油箱
Tao Dào 道
tap shuǐlóng tóu 水龙头
tape (cassette) círdài 磁带
tape-recorder lùyīnjī 录音机

c	→ ts
e	→ er
ei	→ ay
ie	→ yeh
ir	→ er
iu	→ yo
o	→ or
ou	→ oh
q	→ ch
ui	→ way
uo	→ war
x	→ sh
z	→ dz
zh	→ j

tariff guān shuì 关税

taste *(noun)* wèir 味儿

can I taste it? kéyi *chángchang* ma? 可以尝尝吗?

taxi chūzū chē 出租车

will you get me a taxi? nǐ néng bāng wǒ jiào liàng chūzū chē ma?

where can I get a taxi? wǒ zài nǎr néng dǎ liàng chūzū chē?

✈ Illegal taxis (**hēidī**) operate in most cities and are best avoided. A registered taxi-driver will always use the meter for journeys. In Beijing, legitimate cabs can be identified by the B after the 京 **jīng** character on the number plate.

---

how much to...? dào...duōshao qián?

---

taxi-driver chūzū chē sījī 出租车司机

tea chá 茶

a cup of tea, please qǐng lái bēi chá

could I have a pot of tea? qǐng lái hú chá

✈ Tea is one of China's gifts to the world and there are many types, with green tea being by far the commonest. You could try:

black tea hóngchá 红茶

green tea lǜchá 绿茶

scented tea huāchá 花茶

oolong tea *(semi-fermented)* wūlóngchá 乌龙茶

jasmine tea mòlì huāchá 茉莉花茶

chrysanthemum tea júhuāchá 菊花茶

✈ Restaurants usually include tea in the price of a meal. To show the waiters that you

need a refill, place the teapot lid in an open position. Unless you are in a very westernized environment, tea with milk is going to be an extremely odd request. If that's what you want, then say:
with milk jiā niúnǎi 加牛奶

teacher lǎoshīʀ 老师
telephone diànhuà 电话
telephone directory diànhuà bù 电话簿
television diànshìʀ 电视
  I'd like to watch television wó xiǎng kàn diànshìʀ
tell: could you tell me where...? nǐ néng gàosù wǒ nǎr...? 你能告诉我哪儿…?
  could you tell him...? néng gàosu ta...ma?
  I told him that... wǒ gàosu tā...
temperature (weather etc) qìwēn 气温
  he's got a temperature tā fāshāo le 他发烧了
temple miào 庙
Temple of Heaven Tiāntán 天坛
tennis wǎngqiú 网球
tennis ball wǎngqiú 网球
tennis court wǎngqiú chǎng 网球场
tennis racket wǎngqiú pāi 网球拍
tent zhàngpeng 帐篷
terminus zhōngdiǎn zhàn 终点站
terracotta warriors bīngmǎyǒng 兵马俑
terrible zhēn zāogāo 真糟糕
terrific bàngjíle 棒极了
text: I'll text you wǒ géi nǐ fā *duǎnxìn* 我给你发短信
text message duǎnxìn 短信
Thailand Tàiguó 泰国
than bǐ 比

c	→ ts
e	→ er
ei	→ ay
ie	→ yeh
iʀ	→ yeh
iu	→ yo
o	→ or
ou	→ oh
q	→ ch
ui	→ way
uo	→ war
x	→ sh
z	→ dz
zh	→ j

bigger than... bǐ...dà 比…大

> Note the Chinese word order.
>
> **wó bǐ tā gāo**
> I am taller than her
> *(literally: I than her tall)*

thanks, thank you xièxie 谢谢
thank you very much fēicháng gǎnxiè 非常感谢
no thank you bú yào, xièxie
thank you for your help xièxie nǐ de bāngzhù

> *YOU MAY THEN HEAR*
> bú yòng kèqi *you're welcome*

that nèige 那个
that man/table nèige nánde/zhuōzɪʀ
I would like that one wǒ yào nèige
and that? nèige ne?
I think that... wó xiǎng... 我想…
the

> Chinese does not have (or need) a word
> for 'the' (or 'a'). So:
>
> **get the police** **opposite the hotel**
> jiào jǐngchá fàndiàn duìmiàn
> *(literally: get police)* *(literally: hotel opposite)*

theatre jòyʊàn 剧院
their tāmen de 他们的
theirs: it's theirs zhè shɪʀ tāmen de 这是他们的
them *(persons)* tāmen 他们
(objects) tāmen 它们
for them gěi tāmen

> When 'them' refers to objects it is usually
> omitted in Chinese.

> **wó xǐhuān**
> I like them (literally: I like)

then (at that time) nà shíʀhou 那时候
  (after that) ránhòu 然后
there nàr 那儿
  how do I get there? wó zěnme dào nàr?
  is there/are there...? yǒu...ma? 有 … 吗？
  there is/there are... yǒu...
  there isn't/there aren't... méiyou... 没有 …
  there you are (giving something) géi nǐ 给你
these zhèixiē 这些
  these apples zhèixiē píngguǒ
  can I take these? wǒ néng ná zhèixie ma?
they tāmen 他们

> If 'they' refers to objects, Chinese
> normally does not translate it.
>
> **they are broken**
> huàile (literally: broken)

thick hòu 厚
  (stupid) bèn 笨
thief zéi 贼
thigh dàtuǐ 大腿
thin (cloth) báo 薄
  (person) shòu 瘦
  (line) xì 细
thing (object) dōngxi 东西
  (matter) shìʀ 事
  I've lost all my things wǒ de dōngxi
  dōu diū le
think xiǎng 想
  I'll think it over wó hǎohāo
  xiángxiang
  I think so wó xiǎng shìʀ zhèiyang
  I don't think so wó xiǎng búshìʀ

c	→	ts
e	→	er
ei	→	ay
ie	→	yeh
iʀ	→	er
iu	→	yo
o	→	or
ou	→	oh
q	→	ch
ui	→	way
uo	→	war
x	→	sh
z	→	dz
zh	→	j

third *(adjective)* dìsān 第三

thirsty: I'm thirsty wó kě le 我渴了

this zhèige 这个

　this hotel/this street zhèige fàndiàn/zhè tiáo jiē

　can I have this one? wǒ néng yào zhèige ma?

　this is my wife/this is Mr... zhè shìr wǒ qīzir/zhè shìr...xiānsheng 这是我妻子/这是…先生

　this is very good zhè hén hǎo 这很好

　this is... *(on telephone)* wǒ shìr... 我是…

　is this...? zhè shìr...ma?

　and this? zhèige ne?

those nàxiē 那些

　no, not these, those! bú shìr, bú shìr zhèixiē, shìr nàxiē

　how much are those? nàxiē duōshao qián?

thread *(noun)* xiàn 线

throat sǎngzir 嗓子

throttle *(of motorbike, boat)* yóuménr 油门儿

through *(across)* jīngguò 经过

　through Shanghai jīngguò Shànghǎi

　it's through there jiù zài nàr 就在那儿

throw *(verb)* rēng 扔

thumb dà múzhǐr 大拇指

thunder *(noun)* léi 雷

thunderstorm léiyǔ 雷雨

Thursday xīngqī sìr 星期四

Tibet Xīzàng 西藏

ticket piào 票

tie *(necktie)* lǐngdài 领带

tiger láohǔ 老虎

tight *(clothes)* jǐn 紧

tights *(pair)* liánkù wà 连裤袜

time shírjiān 时间

　I haven't got time wǒ méi shírjiān

　for the time being zànshír 暂时

this time/last time/next time zhè cìr/shàng cìr/xià cìr 这次 / 上次 / 下次

three times sāncìr

have a good time! wánr de hǎo! 玩儿得好!

what's the time? jídiǎn le? 几点了？

➔ The clocks don't change for summer time, and the whole country uses Beijing time, despite the difference in the time of sunset and sunrise between the far east and the far west of the country. The 24-hour system is used for timetables.

HOW TO TELL THE TIME

it's 3 o'clock sān diǎn le

it's 6 o'clock liù diǎn le

it's 10 past 3 sān diǎn shír fēn *(literally: 3 o'clock 10 minutes)*

it's quarter past 3 sān diǎn yíkè

it's half past 3 sān diǎn bàn

it's 20 to 4 sìr diǎn chà èrshír

it's quarter to 4 sìr diǎn chà yíkè

---

timetable shírkè biǎo 时刻表

tin *(can)* guàntou 罐头

tin-opener guàntou qǐzir 罐头起子

tip xiǎofèi 小费

is the tip included? bāokuò xiǎofèi ma?

➔ Tipping is not necessary or expected in bars, restaurants or taxis. Hotels are different.

tired lèi 累

I'm tired wǒ lèi le

tissues zhǐrjīn 纸巾

to dào 到

c	→	ts
e	→	er
ei	→	ay
ie	→	yeh
iʀ	→	er
iu	→	yo
o	→	or
ou	→	oh
q	→	ch
ui	→	way
uo	→	war
x	→	sh
z	→	dz
zh	→	j

to Shanghai dào Shànghǎi 到上海
to Xiao Ming's dào Xiǎo Míng de jiā
go to **time**

toast *(piece of)* kǎo miànbāo piàn 烤面包片

tobacco yān 烟

today jīntiān 今天

toe jiǎo zhǐtou 脚指头

tofu dòufu 豆腐

together yíkuàir 一块儿
we're together wǒmen shìr yíkuàir de
can we pay all together? wǒmen kéyi yíkuàir
fù ma?

toilet cèsuǒ 厕所
where are the toilets? cèsuǒ zài nǎr?
I have to go to the toilet wó bìxū qù cèsuǒ

✈ It's a good idea to carry tissues with you;
most public toilets don't have toilet paper.

---

toilet paper: there's no toilet paper méiyǒu
shóuzhǐr 没有手纸

tomato xīhóngshìr 西红柿

tomato juice fānqié zhǐr 蕃茄汁

tomato ketchup fānqié jiàng 蕃茄酱

tomorrow míngtiān 明天
tomorrow morning míngtiān shàngwu
tomorrow afternoon míngtiān xiàwu
tomorrow evening míngtiān wǎnshang
the day after tomorrow hòutiān 后天
see you tomorrow míngtiān jiàn

tongue shétou 舌头

tonic (water) tānglì shuǐ 汤力水

tonight jīn wǎn 今晚

tonsillitis biǎntáoxiàn yán 扁桃腺炎

too tài 太
(also) yě 也
that's too much nà tài duō le

me too wó yě shìr

tool gōngjù 工具

tooth yá 牙

toothache: I've got toothache wǒ yá téng
我牙疼

toothbrush yáshuā 牙刷

toothpaste yágāo 牙膏

top: on top of zài...shàngtou 在…上头
 on the top floor zài *dǐng* céng 在顶层
 at the top zài dǐng shang

torch shǒudiàn tǒng 手电筒

total *(noun)* zǒngshù 总数

tough *(meat)* lǎo 老

tour *(noun)* yóulǎn 游览
 (of museum, gallery) cānguān 参观
 we'd like to go on a tour of... wǒmen xiǎng
 yóulǎn...
 we'd like to go on a tour of the island
 wǒmen xiǎng yóulǎn zhèige dǎo
 we're touring around wǒmen zhuànzhuan
 我们转转

tourist yóukè 游客
 I'm a tourist wǒ shìr yóukè

tourist office lǚyóu zīrxún zhōngxīn
 旅游咨询中心

tow tuō 拖

towards cháozhe 朝着

towel máojīn 毛巾

town chéngzhèn 城镇
 in town zài chéng lǐr 在城里
 would you take me into town? nǐ
 néng dài wǒ jìn chéng ma?

traditional chuántǒng 传统
 a traditional Chinese meal chuántǒng
 de Zhōngguó fàn

traffic jiāotōng 交通

c	→	ts
e	→	er
ei	→	ay
ie	→	yeh
iʀ	→	er
iu	→	yo
o	→	or
ou	→	oh
q	→	ch
ui	→	way
uo	→	war
x	→	sh
z	→	dz
zh	→	j

traffic jam jiāotōng dǔsè 交通堵塞
traffic lights hónglǜ dēng 红绿灯
train huǒchē 火车

✈ To avoid queuing, it is easier to get train tickets from your hotel's travel office than from the station. There are also many train ticket sales offices (铁路售票处 **tiělù shòupiào chù**) in cities. Best to book in advance as train travel is very popular. Remember that there are no return tickets and that your ticket will only be valid for the time printed on it (but you can get a ticket altered). The most comfortable way to travel is
soft seat ruǎnzuò 软座
or
soft sleeper ruǎnwò 软卧
Otherwise there is the cheaper (and crowded)
hard seat yìngzuò 硬座
or
hard sleeper yìngwò 硬卧

I'd like a ticket to... wǒ xiǎng yào yì zhāng qù...de piào
I'd like two tickets to... wó xiǎng yào liǎng zhāng qù...de piào
for tomorrow at 12.30 míngtiān shír'èr diǎn bàn

trainers yùndòng xié 运动鞋
train station huǒchē zhàn 火车站
tranquillizers zhènjìng jì 镇静剂
translate fānyì 翻译
   would you translate that for me? nǐ néng géi wǒ fānyì yíxia ma?

travel lǚxíng 旅行
travel agent's lǚxíng shè 旅行社
traveller's cheque lǚxíng zhīpiào 旅行支票

✈ Not widely recognized in China.

tree shù 树
tremendous (very good) hǎojíle 好极了
trim: just a trim, please qíng zhǐr xiūxiu 请只
修修
trip (journey) lǚxíng 旅行
(outing) wánr 玩儿
we want to go on a trip to... wǒmen xiǎng
qù...wánr
trouble wèntí 问题
I'm having trouble with... wó yǒu...de wèntí
trousers kùzir 裤子
true zhēn 真
it's not true bú shìr zhēn de
trunks (swimming) yóuyǒng kù 游泳裤
try shìrshir 试试
can I try it on? wǒ kéyi shìrshir ma?
T-shirt tì xù shān T 恤衫
Tuesday xīngqī èr 星期二
tunnel suìdào 隧道
turn: where do we turn off? wǒmen zài
nǎr guǎiwān? 我们在哪儿拐弯？
twice liǎngcìr 两次
twice as much liǎng bèi 两倍
twin beds liǎngge dānrén chuáng 两个
单人床
twin room shuāngrén jiān 双人间
typical diǎnxíng 典型
tyre lúntāi 轮胎
I need a new tyre wǒ xūyào ge xīn
lúntāi

c	→ ts
e	→ er
ei	→ ay
ie	→ yeh
iʀ	→ yo
iu	→ yo
o	→ or
ou	→ oh
q	→ ch
ui	→ way
uo	→ war
x	→ sh
z	→ dz
zh	→ j

U

ugly nánkàn 难看

ulcer kuìyáng 溃疡

umbrella yúsǎn 雨伞

uncle: my uncle (father's brother) wǒ shūshu 我叔叔

(mother's brother) wǒ jiùjiu 我舅舅

uncomfortable bù shūfu 不舒服

unconscious bù xǐng rénshìʀ 不省人事

he's unconscious tā bù xǐng rénshìʀ

under zài...dǐxia 在…底下

(less than) yǐxià 以下

underdone bàn shēng bù shú 半生不熟

underground (rail) dìtiě 地铁

✈ Several cities have undergrounds. There is usually a flat rate for any journey.

understand: I understand wó dǒng le 我懂了

I don't understand wǒ bù dǒng

do you understand? ní dǒng ma?

undo jiěkāi 解开

unfriendly bù yóuhǎo 不友好

unhappy bù gāoxìng 不高兴

United States Měiguó 美国

university dàxʋé 大学

unlock kāi 开

until zhírdào 直到

until next year zhírdào xià yìnián

not until Tuesday zhírdào xīngqī èr cái 直到星期二才

unusual bù píngcháng 不平常

up shàng 上

he's not up yet tā hái méi qǐlai 他还没起来

what's up? zěnme le? 怎么了？

up there zài nàr 在那儿

upside-down dào le 倒了

upstairs lóushang 楼上

urgent jí 急

us wǒmen 我们

  it's us shìr wǒmen

  for us wèi wǒmen

USA Měiguó 美国

use: can I use...? wǒ kéyi yòng...ma? 我可以用…吗?

useful yǒuyòng 有用

usual píngcháng 平常

  as usual xiàng píngcháng yíyàng

usually píngcháng 平常

V

vacate (*room*) bānchū 搬出

vacation jiàqī 假期

vaccination dǎ yùfáng zhēn 打预防针

vacuum flask rèshuǐ píng 热水瓶

valid yǒuxiào 有效

  how long is it valid for? duō cháng shíjiān nèi yǒuxiào?

valley shāngǔ 山谷

valuable guìzhòng 贵重

  will you look after my valuables? nǐ néng báoguǎn wǒ de guìzhòng wùpǐn ma?

value jiàzhír 价值

van xiǎo huòchē 小货车

vanilla xiāngcǎo 香草

vegetables shūcài 蔬菜

vegetarian sùshír zhě 素食者

ventilator páiqì shàn 排气扇

very hěn 很

c	→ ts
e	→ er
ei	→ ay
ie	→ yeh
iʀ	→ er
iu	→ yo
o	→ or
ou	→ oh
q	→ ch
ui	→ way
uo	→ war
x	→ sh
z	→ dz
zh	→ j

very much hěn

via jīngguò 经过

video lùxiàng 录像

Vietnam Yuènán 越南

village cūnziʀ 村子

vinegar cù 醋

virus bìngdú 病毒

visa qiānzhèng 签证

visit *(person)* kàn 看
   (museum etc) cānguān 参观

vodka fútèjiā jiǔ 伏特加酒

voice shēngyīn 声音

voltage diànyā 电压

✈ 220 volts as in the UK.

W

waist yāo 腰

wait: will we have to wait long? wǒmen yào *děng* hénjiǔ ma? 我们要等很久吗？
   wait for me děng zhe wǒ
   I'm waiting for a friend/my wife wǒ zài děng ge péngyou/wǒ tàitai

waiter fúwù yuán 服务员
   waiter! fúwù yuán!

waitress fúwù yuán 服务员

wake: will you wake me up at 7.30? nǐ néng qī diǎn bàn *jiào xǐng* wǒ ma? 你能7点半叫醒我吗？

Wales Wēi'ěrshìʀ 威尔士

walk: can we walk there? wǒmen néng *zǒu* dào nàr ma? 我们能走到那儿吗？

wall qiáng 墙

wallet qiánbāo 钱包

want: I want... wǒ yào... 我要…

I want to talk to... wǒ yào hé … shuōhuà

what do you want? nǐ yào shénme?

I don't want to wǒ bú yào

he/she wants to... tā yào...

war zhànzhēng 战争

warm nuǎnhuo 暖和

warning jǐnggào 警告

was go to be

wash: can you wash these for me? nǐ néng gěi wǒ xǐ zhèixiē ma? 你能给我洗这些吗？

washbasin xíshǒu chír 洗手池

washing machine xǐyī jī 洗衣机

washing powder xǐyī fěn 洗衣粉

wasp huángfēng 黄蜂

watch *(wristwatch)* shóubiǎo 手表

  will you watch my bags for me? nǐ néng kān wǒ de bāo ma? 你能看我的包吗？

  watch out! xiǎoxīn! 小心！

water shuǐ 水

  can I have some water? qǐng lái diánr shuǐ

  hot and cold running water lěng rè shuǐ

✈ Tap water is not for drinking. Instead, the Chinese drink boiled water (kept in thermos flasks) or bottled mineral water.

c	→	ts
e	→	er
ei	→	ay
ie	→	yeh
iʀ	→	er
iu	→	yo
o	→	or
ou	→	oh
q	→	ch
ui	→	way
uo	→	war
x	→	sh
z	→	dz
zh	→	j

---

waterfall pùbù 瀑布

waterproof fángshuǐ 防水

way: it's this way shìr zhèitiáo lù 是这条路

  it's that way shìr nèitiáo lù

  do it this way zhèiyang zuò 这样做

  no way! méi ménr! 没门儿！

  is it on the way to...? zhè shìr qù ...fāngxiàng de lù ma? 这是去…方向的路吗？

  could you tell me the way to get

to...? néng gàosu wǒ dào...de lù ma?
go to **where** *for answers*

we wǒmen 我们

we are English wǒmen shìʀ Yīngguó rén

weak *(person)* ruò 弱

weather tiānqì 天气

    what filthy weather! zhè tiānqì zhēn zāo!

    what's the weather forecast? tiānqì yùbào
shuō shénme?

YOU MAY THEN HEAR
jiāng huì yóu yǔ *it's going to rain*
tiānqì qíng *it'll be sunny*
tiānqì zhuǎn qíng *it'll clear up*

---

website wǎngzhàn 网站

Wednesday xīngqī sān 星期三

week xīngqī 星期

    a week today xiàge xīngqi de jīntiān

    a week tomorrow xiàge xīngqi de míngtiān

weekend: at the weekend zhōumò 周末

weight zhòngliàng 重量

welcome: you're welcome búxiè 不谢

well: I'm not feeling well wǒ bù shūfu 我不舒服

    he's not well tā bù shūfu

    how are you? – very well, thanks ní hǎo ma?
– hén hǎo, xièxie 你好吗？- 很好, 谢谢

    you speak English very well nǐ Yīngyǔ jiǎngde
hén hǎo

    well, well! hǎo ba 好吧

Welsh Wēi'ěrshìʀ 威尔士

were *go to* **be**

west xī 西

    in the West zài xī fāng

West Indies Xī Yìndù Qúndǎo 西印度群岛

wet shìʀ 湿

    (weather) xiàyǔ 下雨

what? shénme? 什么？
  what is that? nà shìʀ shénme?
  what for? wèi shénme?
  what train? shénme huǒchē?
wheel lúnziʀ 轮子
wheel chair lúnyǐ 轮椅
when? shénme shíʀhou? 什么时候？
  when is breakfast? zǎofàn zài shénme shíʀhou?
  when we arrived dāng wǒmen dào de shíʀhou 当我们到的时候
where? nǎr? 哪儿？
  where is...?...zài nǎr?

> *YOU MAY THEN HEAR*
> yìzhíʀ zǒu *go straight on*
> xiàng zuǒ/yòu zhuǎn *turn left/right*
> dào dì èr ge shíʀziʀ lùkou *go as far as the second crossroads*
> zài nàr *down there*
> huídào *go back to*
> guò le *go past*

which nǎge 哪个
  (with plural) nǎxiē 哪些
  which one? nǎge?

> *YOU MAY THEN HEAR*
> zhèige *this one*
> nèige *that one*
> nèi biānr de nèige *that one over there*

whisky wēishìʌjì 威士忌
white báisè 白色
white wine bái pútaojiǔ 白葡萄酒
who? shéi? 谁？
whose: whose is this? zhè shìʀ shéide? 这是谁的？

c	→ ts
e	→ er
ei	→ ay
ie	→ yeh
iʀ	→ er
iu	→ yo
o	→ or
ou	→ oh
q	→ ch
ui	→ way
uo	→ war
x	→ sh
z	→ dz
zh	→ j

> *YOU MAY THEN HEAR*
> shìr wǒ de *it's mine*
> shìr nǐ de/tā de *it's yours/his/hers*

why? wèishénme 为什么？
  why not? wèishénme bù?

> *YOU MAY THEN HEAR*
> yīnwei *because*

wide kuān 宽
wife: my wife wǒ tàitai 我太太
will: when will it be finished? shénme shírhou
wán? 什么时候完？
  will you do it? nǐ *néng* zuò ma? 你能做吗？
  I'll come back wǒ *huì* huílai de 我会回来的

> Chinese does not have tenses. Context is
> normally enough to make it clear whether
> you are talking about the future.
>
> **wǒmen míngtiān zǒu**
> we're leaving tomorrow
>
> But you can use **huì** to indicate the future.

win yíng 赢
  who won? shéi yíng le?
wind *(noun)* fēng 风
window chuānghu 窗户
  near the window kào chuānghu
window seat kào chuānghu de zuòwèi 靠窗户
的座位
windscreen dǎngfēng bōli 挡风玻璃
windscreen wipers yǔ cā 雨擦
windy yǒu fēng 有风
wine pútaojiǔ 葡萄酒
  can I see the wine list? wǒ néng kàn *jiǔdān*
ma? 我能看酒单吗？

✈ Chinese wine is sold in many restaurants.

two red wines liǎng bēi hóng pútaojiǔ

winter dōngtian 冬天
wire tiěsī 铁丝
  (electric) diànxiàn 电线
wish: best wishes zhù hǎo 祝好
with gēn 跟
  with me gēn wǒ yìqǐ
without méiyǒu 没有
  without sugar méiyǒu táng
witness *(of accident etc)* zhèngrén 证人
  will you act as a witness for me? nǐ néng dāng wǒ de zhèngrén ma?
wok guō 锅
woman nǚrén 女人
  women nǚrén
wonderful hǎojíle 好极了
won't: it won't start bù qǐdòng 不起动
wood mùtou 木头
  (forest) shùlín 树林
wool yángmáo 羊毛
word cír 词
work gōngzuò 工作
  I work in London wǒ zài Lúndūn gōngzuò
  it's not working bù líng le 不灵了
work permit gōngzuò xǔ kě 工作许可
world shìjiè 世界
  the whole world zhěng gè shìjiè
worry: I'm worried about him wǒ wèi tā dānxīn 我为他担心
  don't worry bié dānxīn
worse: it's worse nà gèng zāo 那更糟
worst zuì zāo 最糟

c	→ ts
e	→ er
ei	→ ay
ie	→ yeh
iʀ	→ er
iu	→ yo
o	→ or
ou	→ oh
q	→ ch
ui	→ way
uo	→ war
x	→ sh
z	→ dz
zh	→ j

worth: it's not worth that much bù *zhír* nàme duō qián 不值那么多钱

worthwhile: is it worthwhile going to...? *zhír de* qù...ma? 值得去…吗?

wrap: could you wrap it up? néng bǎ tā *bāo* qǐlai ma? 能把它包起来吗?

wrench *(tool)* bānshǒu 扳手

wrist shǒuwàn 手腕

write xiě 写

could you write it down? nǐ néng bǎ tā xiě xiàlai ma?

writing paper xìnzhǐʀ 信纸

wrong cuò le 错了

I think the bill's wrong wǒ juéde zhàngdān cuò le

there's something wrong with... ...yǒu wèntí …有问题

you're wrong nǐ cuò le

that's the wrong key zhè yàoshiʀ *bú duì* 这钥匙不对

sorry, wrong number duìbuqǐ, dǎ cuò le

I got the wrong train wǒ shàng cuò huǒchē le 我上错火车了

what's wrong? zěnme le? 怎么了?

Y

yacht yóutǐng 游艇

Yangtze River Chángjiāng 长江

yard

 1 yard = 91.44 cms = 0.91 m

year nián 年

this year jīn nián

next year míng nián

yellow huángsè 黄色

yellow pages huáng yè 黄页
Yellow River Huánghé 黄河
Yellow Sea Huánghǎi 黄海
yes shìʀ 是

Although you could use **shìr**, the natural Chinese way of saying 'yes' is to repeat the verb in the question.

nǐ lái ma?	**lái**
are you coming?	yes *(literally: come)*

ní yǒu...ma?	**yǒu**
do you have...?	yes *(literally: have)*

You can also use **duì** (correct).

nǐ zài xʋé Zhōngwén ma?
are you learning Chinese?

duì
yes, I am; that's right

To go along with a suggestion you can use **hǎo**.

**wǒmen hē diǎnr   hǎo
shénme ba?**
let's have a drink   yes; right; OK

To disagree with someone:

you can't – yes, I can
nǐ bù xíng – bù, wǒ xíng

Here Chinese says 'no, I can' ie 'no, I disagree with what you say, I can'.

c	→ **ts**
e	→ **er**
ei	→ **ay**
ie	→ **yeh**
iʀ	→ **er**
iu	→ **yo**
o	→ **or**
ou	→ **oh**
q	→ **ch**
ui	→ **way**
uo	→ **war**
x	→ **sh**
z	→ **dz**
zh	→ **j**

yesterday zuótiān 昨天
  the day before yesterday qiántiān 前天
  yesterday morning zuótiān shàngwu
  yesterday afternoon zuótiān xiàwu

yet: is it ready yet? hǎo le ma? 好了吗？
  not yet hái méiyou 还没有
yoghurt suānnǎi 酸奶
yoghurt drink rǔsuān yǐnliào 乳酸饮料

> ✈ Drinking yoghurt, drunk with straws from
> ceramic pots, is widely available from
> street stalls and small shops.

you nǐ 你
  (polite form) nín 您
  (plural) nǐmen 你们
  I like you wó xǐhuān nǐ
  is that you? shìr nǐ ma?

> Use the polite form to a more senior
> person. When talking to (or about)
> people you can also use the words **xiǎo** +
> surname (for younger people) and **lǎo** +
> surname (for older people).
>   **how are you, Zhou?**
>   ní hǎo ma, xiǎo Zhōu?

young niánqīng 年青
your, yours nǐ de 你的
  (polite form) nín de 您的
  (of several people) nǐmen de 你们的
  your car/son nǐ de chē/ érziʀ
  is this yours? zhè shìr nǐ de ma?

Z

zero líng 零
  below zero líng dù yǐxià 零度以下
zip lāliàn 拉链
  could you put a new zip on? nǐ néng bāng
  wǒ huàn ge lāliàn ma ?
zoo dòngwù yuán 动物园

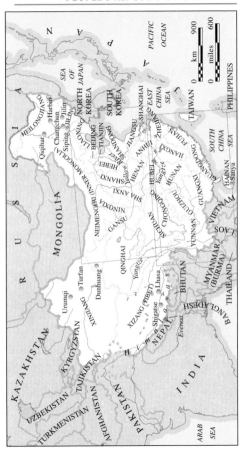

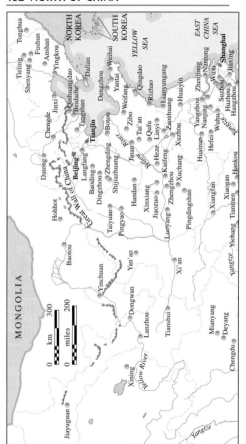

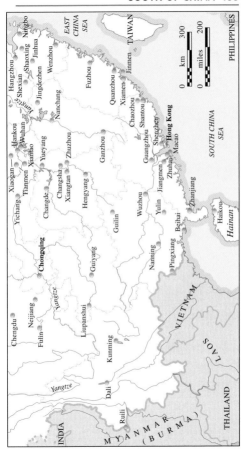

爱护公共财物	àihù gōnggòng cáiwù *protect public property*
保持安静	bǎochí ānjìng *silence*
办公时间	bàngōng shíjiān *office hours*
职工专用	zhígōng zhuānyòng *staff only*
不准垂钓	bùzhǔn chuídiào *no fishing*
出口	chūkǒu *exit*
此路不通	cǐlù bùtōng *dead end*
存包处	cúnbāo chù *cloakroom*
存车处	cúnchē chù *bike parking*
单行线	dān xíng xiàn *one way*
电梯	diàntī *lift*
妇女、儿童优先	fùnǚ, értóng yōuxiān *women and children first*
公厕	gōng cè *public toilets*
关	guān *off*

禁区	jìn qū *restricted area*
禁止打猎	jìnzhǐʀ dǎliè *no hunting*
禁止入内	jìnzhǐʀ rùnèi *no entry*
禁止驶入	jìnzhǐʀ shǐʀrù *no entry*
禁止停车	jìnzhǐʀ tíngchē *no parking*
禁止通行	jìnzhǐʀ tōngxíng *road closed*
禁止吸烟	jìnzhǐʀ xīyān *no smoking*
禁止携犬入内	jìnzhǐʀ xiéquǎn rùnèi *dogs not allowed*
开	kāi *on*
靠右	kào yòu *keep right*
靠左	kào zuǒ *keep left*
拉	lā *pull*
慢驶	màn shǐʀ *slow*
免费入场	miǎnfèi rùchǎng *admission free*

男厕（所）	nán cè(suǒ) *gents*
女厕（所）	nǚ cè(suǒ) *ladies*
请勿拍照	qǐng wù pāizhào *no photos*
请勿随地吐痰	qǐng wù súidì tǔtán *no spitting*
请勿吸烟	qǐng wù xīyān *no smoking*
请勿用手摸	qǐng wù yòng shǒu mō *please do not touch*
前面施工	qiánmiàn shīrgōng *road works ahead*
切勿近火	qiè wù jìn huǒ *keep away from fire*
入口	rù kǒu *entrance*
生产日期	shēngchǎn rìrqī *date of manufacture*
失效期	shīr xiào qī *expiry date, best before*
售票处	shòupiào chù *ticket office*
恕不出售	shù bù chūshòu *not for sale*
停止营业	tíngzhǐr yíngyè *closed*
推	tuī *push*

危险	wēixiǎn *danger*
问讯处	wènxùn chù *information*
勿乱扔杂物	wù luànrēng záwù *no litter*
无人	wú rén *vacant, free*
小心路滑	xiǎoxīn lù huá *slippery road surface*
闲人免进	xiánrén miǎn jìn *staff only*
行李存放处	xíngli cúnfàng chù *left luggage*
休息	xiūxi *closed*
一慢，二看， 三通过	yī màn, èr kàn, sān tōngguò *slow down, look, then cross*
营业	yíngyè *open*
营业时间	yíngyè shíjiān *business hours*
有人	yǒu rén *engaged, occupied*
油漆未干	yóuqī wèi gān *wet paint*
游人止步	yóurén zhǐr bù *private grounds*

0	líng	〇
1	yī	一
2	èr or liǎng*	二 or 两
3	sān	三
4	sìR	四
5	wǔ	五
6	liù	六
7	qī	七
8	bā	八
9	jiǔ	九
10	shíR	十

For 11-19 you take the word for 10 and add the unit.

11	shíRyī	十一
12	shíR'èr	十二
13	shíRsān	十三

For 20, 30, 40 etc you place the unit in front of the word for 10.

20	èrshíR	二十
30	sānshíR	三十
40	sìRshíR	四十

The same patterns apply for multiples of 10 plus units.

21	èrshíRyī	二十一
58	wǔshíRbā	五十八
99	jiǔshíRjiǔ	九十九

And then likewise with the hundreds.

100	yìbǎi	一百
200	èrbǎi, liángbǎi	二百, 两百
300	sānbǎi	三百
480	sìRbǎi bāshíR	四百八十

In numbers like 108, 109 etc Chinese spells out the 0 or **líng** (like saying one hundred o eight). Also with the numbers 11-19, when used after a hundred, **yī** is inserted.

108	yìbǎi líng bā	一百零八
312	sānbǎi yī shír'èr	三百一十二

A thousand is **qiān** 千.

1,000	yìqiān	一千
2,000	liǎngqiān	两千
3,000	sānqiān	三千
5,670	wǔqiān liùbǎi qī shíR	五千六百七十

There's a special word for 10,000: **wàn** 万.

10,000	yīwàn	一万
33,000	sānwàn sānqiān	三万三千

(This is literally: three 10,000 + 3,000)

100,000	shírwàn	十万
10,000,000	yìqiānwàn	一千万

A million (not a Chinese unit) is said as a hundred ten thousands.

1,000,000	yìbǎiwàn	一百万

There's a special word for 100,000,000 (a hundred million) **yì** 亿.

You'll find the following alternative more complex characters used on bills etc.

0	líng	零	**7**	qī	柒
1	yī	壹	**8**	bā	捌
2	èr	贰	**9**	jiǔ	玖
3	sān	叁	**10**	shíR	拾
4	sìR	肆	**100**	bǎi	佰
5	wǔ	伍	**1,000**	qiān	仟
6	liù	陆			

Ordinal numbers

Ordinal numbers are formed by putting **dì** in front of the cardinal numbers.

1	yī	一
1st	dìyī	第一

2	èr	二
2nd	dì'èr	第二

Classifiers or measure words

If you are using numbers to count people or things, as opposed to just giving a phone number or a price etc, then you have to insert an additional classifier or measure word (like 'two *loaves* of bread' in English). There is a range of classifiers, used for different types of objects. One which will often work is **ge**.

three people
sān ge rén

four bowls
sìR ge wǎn

Days, nights and years don't need classifiers.

three nights
sān wǎn

*Of the words for the number 2 **liǎng** is the only one that you can use with a classifier.

room 22
èrshí'èr hào fángjiān

but

two people
liǎng ge rén